LONDON
IN COLOUR

LONDON
IN COLOUR

A Collection of
Colour Photographs by

JAMES RIDDELL

With an Introductory Text
and Notes on the Illustrations by

WILLIAM GAUNT

LONDON

B. T. BATSFORD LIMITED

First published 1955

PRINTED AND BOUND IN GREAT BRITAIN
BY JARROLD AND SONS LTD, LONDON AND NORWICH
FOR THE PUBLISHERS
B. T. BATSFORD LTD.
4 FITZHARDINGE STREET, PORTMAN SQUARE, LONDON, W.1

CONTENTS

LIST OF ILLUSTRATIONS

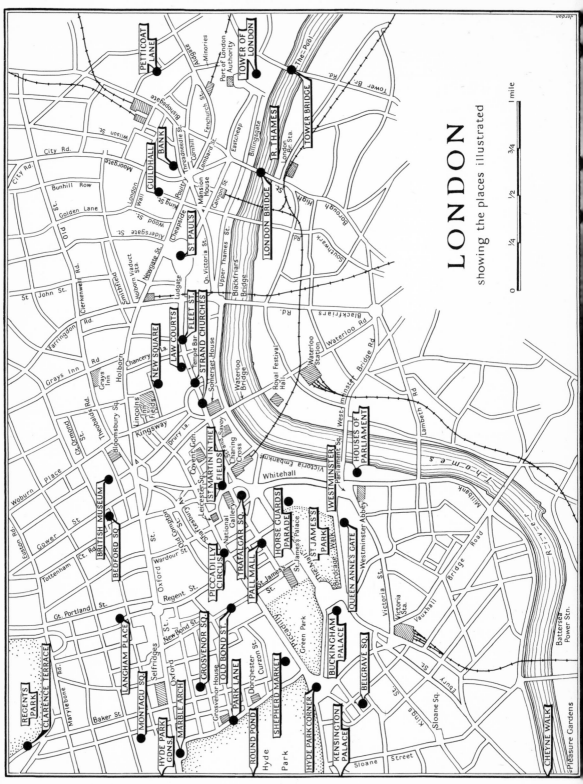

LONDON

showing the places illustrated

0   ¼   ½   ¾   1 mile

8

I The Colour of London

FROM its best-known buildings, stateliest thoroughfares and regions of historic interest to its obscurest nooks and by-ways, London, in the second half of the twentieth century. can be viewed with fresh enjoyment. The year of Coronation, 1953, gives a definite date by which one could say that the capital had at last shed the layers of war-time disguise. The sombre make-up of the blackout was a memory; gone were the sooty sandbags that in the course of years seemed to have incorporated themselves with the architecture; sprayed, scraped, repaired, the long-neglected façades took on a sparkle of well-being; ceasing to be cavities of fantastic ruin, the gaps caused by bombing became the tidy ground-plan of new development. The old London, fortunately including the greater landmarks and places of pilgrimage, survives, yet the face of the city changes; it is, at once, old, rejuvenated and new.

Colour is a decided element in this new-old personality, a subtle blend of various ingredients. To say that London is a grey city is not untrue but is only a part or an imperfect statement of a truth. Its grey is a whole gamut, sometimes as tender and opalescent as at others it is severe, warm as well as cold, verging gaily on white and again deepening into romantic darkness; an even tone only when one ceases to think of any particular view and merely contemplates, as an enormous generalisation, its thirty and more miles from east to west, its twenty miles and more from north to south.

Constituents in this variety are climate, architecture, the expression of the twentieth-century taste for bright hues, and the tide of life itself. Climate being the factor least liable to change, many of its effects are as they always were. The mildly vaporous air of London creates its own schemes of colour and light. The early morning mist in St. James's Park gives its suggestion of almost Chinese landscape. A pale golden sunlight, throwing no shadows, such as Joseph Conrad described in *The Secret Agent*, pervades the streets with its mysterious glow; twilight descends on the river in the dusky softness of blue that was Whistler's special discovery. Because there is on the whole less smoke, the atmosphere seems not so dense as it used to be. It is only by a rare and impish trick of nature that visitors from France are confronted by the pea-soup fog that tradition has taught them to expect. Its reappearance in the acute and disastrous form of "smog" was the rarest of modern freaks. Very remote, to speak broadly, is the pall of bilious green that so often shrouded the London of the eighties. A foggy day, in the moderate sense and of less than pea-soup density has, it is true, much colour to commend it. There was, in the nineteen-twenties, an Italian artist who used to paint in the streets of London and greet such a day with delight as the best for his purpose. He explained with some plausibility that there was greater richness in the particle-laden atmosphere than under the clear sky of his native place; yet the dwindling of these riches can scarcely be regretted and though London skies are not Italian, there is a special beauty in the softness and clarity combined that a present-day colour photograph is well fitted to reveal.

With colour atmospheric, colour architectural is wedded, though by no means in monotonous union. There are different strata; the clamorous red of outer suburbs contrasts emphatically with that inner ring of nineteenth-century houses, built with the sober ochreous brick that comes from the London clay, and encircling the varied splendours of the city's core. It is in the central areas, of course, that one can best appreciate the silvery beauty of Portland stone weathering through centuries of London climate to exquisite effect, material with the poetic range of grey that soot, rain and time can only enhance, chosen by Inigo Jones for the Banqueting House, Whitehall, by Sir Christopher Wren for Saint Paul's, by Sir Charles Barry for the Reform Club, Pall Mall. Or the profound warmth of old red brick, mellow and comforting in a Bloomsbury square; with its stern grandeur in the mighty walls that surround the Docks. With less of satirical intention than the *Quarterly Review* in 1826 one may ask also:

> "*But is not our Nash, too, a very great master?*
> *He finds us all brick and he leaves us all plaster.*"

The "stucco" used by John Nash and popularised by him is capable of ageing into shabbiness and cracking squalor, but when renewed what golden elegance it gives, how well it assorts with the palatial aspect of his terraces in Regent's Park!

The renewal of the old is one of the novelties of the new London. A Nash façade smiles again with all the urbaneness of the Regency; sculptured Victorian detail, once amorphous with grime, invites curious appraisal. Carefully restored, every cusp of its war-wrecked, pointed windows, copied in fresh stone, the wishfully-mediaeval front of a remaining Victorian house in Park Lane gleams as hopefully as if the Gothic Revival was in its heyday. Contributing to the freshness of effect are comparatively new or recent structures that have not lost their pristine quality. Delicately roseate, pastel-tinted, are the fluted chimneys of the Battersea Power Station beneath their Vesuvian cloud. Impeccably white is the Waterloo Bridge that so gracefully clears the muddy Thames, perhaps reconciling the Londoner to the disappearance of the massive and classical old bridge, Sir John Rennie's masterpiece.

Incidental colour constantly catches the eye; in many a side-street or mews, once drab and neglected, but now taken over in the retreat from the great mansions and assuming a Lilliputian smartness, front doors of

lemon, lilac or vermilion, advertise the taste of a colour-conscious genera-
tion. There is a post-war block of flats off Theobald's Road where every
door, on its severe modern balconies, is a note of gaiety and the total result
resembles a picture by Paul Klee. On open spaces—war scars (tended and
healed)—banks of bright flowers are substituted, with an eye to effect, for
the vagrant willow-herb, while of colour that is casual and far from being
the result of a premeditated aesthetic plan there is an abundance.

Consider for instance the prodigious still-lifes of Old Compton Street
in Soho, those dazzling arrays of bottles, cheeses, and cans from all
quarters of the globe . . . during the war there was a wine merchant there
whose strange liqueurs and varied wines were protected with an iron grille
and thus suggested the precious stones in a jeweller's window . . . there,
still, are the emeralds, garnets and chrysoprase of potions that seem to
demand the jewelled vocabulary of a poet of the nineties.

Yet the colour of London can scarcely be considered in the abstract,
it has to be appreciated along with the buildings and their associations,
their connection with the life of the present and the past. For those long
intimate with the city (some of whom, it may be, because of this intimacy
have taken its landmarks for granted) as well as for those who visit it for
the first time, it can be a rewarding experience to begin sight-seeing from
the beginning and to start with the great places of pilgrimage, Westminster
Abbey and St. Paul's, the Houses of Parliament and the Tower of London.

II The Places of Pilgrimage

UNCHANGED externally is the grand historical composition of
Westminster made up of the Abbey, its little companion church,
St. Margaret's, and the "Palace" that comprises the Houses of Parliament.
Westminster Abbey from without has its old, quiet and unspectacular
dignity. Time has welded the western towers into harmony with the rest—
with surprise one remembers that they were once attacked as an un-Gothic
addition to the building. First projected by Sir Christopher Wren, carried
out by Hawksmoor or James in the early eighteenth century, they were
criticised for the intrusion of "a Tuscan cornice", "a Grecian pediment",
yet if one is subconsciously aware of an early Georgian element of style, the
sense of simplicity and dignity remains. The façade of the north transept
bears the mark of restoration at the hands of Gilbert Scott and J. L. Pearson,
but this too is unified with the thirteenth- and fourteenth-century structure
on either side, while Henry VII's Chapel, projecting beyond the apse and
cluster of chapels of the eastern arm, its external tracery cleared of en-
cumbering grime, appears now to advantage as a brilliant Tudor variation

on the Gothic theme: and St. Margaret's, church of the House of Commons, with its early sixteenth-century tower, its late fifteenth-century nave, adds by its small size to the Abbey's impressiveness.

A grey symphony of Gothic in all its phases such, from a purely visual and external view, is Westminster: though the full weight and pressure of history, the beauty of that loftiest of naves, comparable in magnificence with Reims, must, of course, be experienced within the Abbey. It would be outside the scope of this essay to venture down that great perspective from the tomb of Edward the Confessor to the grave of the Unknown Warrior, from Henry VII's Chapel, heraldic with the banners of the Knights of the Bath, superb in its fan-vaulting, to the statuary of Poet's Corner; though it may be remarked that here, too, are "discoveries" to be made. Scarcely until 1945, when the beautiful effigies of Kings and Queens, the stone figures from the chapels of Henry V and Henry VII, were exhibited in the Victoria and Albert Museum, prior to their reinstallation in the Abbey, was it realised that, as the Dean of Westminster put it "in Westminster Abbey we have a treasure-house of sculpture which is perhaps unrivalled". Modern taste, likewise, less apt than a Lord Shelburne's to condemn its memorials of the great from the seventeenth century onwards, as "absurd and inappropriate", has the pleasant task of reappraising the sculpture of a Nicholas Stone, a Rysbrack, a Roubiliac. However, if the main splendour of the Abbey is within, that of St. Paul's Cathedral (tremendous though its interior is) is in full external view, dominant whether one looks down from the height of Hampstead towards the distant misty dome, or across the river from Bankside, or sees it inset behind the railway bridge at Ludgate Circus, or catches delightful and unexpected glimpses of its Baroque detail from the opened spaces to the east.

To see the blue-grey leaded dome on a fine day is to feel, however often the experience is repeated, some access of buoyancy and lightness of heart. The gilt cross (so finely small at a distance yet in fact thirty feet high) flashing in the sun, kindles a spark of cheerfulness; though in all weathers there is reassurance in the effect it gives of serenely and invincibly presiding, so often noted by so many writers. Thus Samuel Butler one stormy day, looking from Waterloo Bridge, through a pall of darkness, remarked how the dome and towers of St. Paul's rose up sharply out of the gloom "looking higher than they actually were and as though they rested upon space". Awesome indeed was this same majesty in 1940, when silhouetted against the red furnace of the blazing City. With unchanging serenity it presides over the changing vistas of post-war.

At closer quarters, the Portland stone, so aptly chosen by Sir Christopher Wren for his masterpiece, reveals its sensitive range of "colour" and chiaroscuro. It makes a varied patina on the double portico of St. Paul's west front with its rows of twin columns (the stone would not permit of huge single columns); tactfully emphasises the delicate proportioning of the two "campanili", or bell-towers, and lends its own touch of composition to the relief in the pediment by Francis Bird, depicting the Conversion of St. Paul. The modern eye is attuned to the Baroque in architecture and sculpture; its feeling for the dramatic; the aesthetic result attained even by what were once thought unscrupulous means. No Pugin now would complain that the outer dome artificially constructed round the inner is a sham and falsehood because not functional; few would greatly deplore the upper story with its blind windows and balcony that serves no purpose save that of simplifying the aspect and hiding unprepossessing buttresses: while the sculptures of Bird and his masters, Caius Cibber and Grinling Gibbons arouse increased interest. These figures of St. Paul (fifteen feet high), flanked by St. Peter and St. James, Cibber's "incense potts", the angels and palm branches, with the royal arms, carved by Gibbons on the north portico, the phoenix rising from the flames on the south, with the word "Resurgam" (that has its present-day point) animate the grey solemnity.

Warm in colour, save when twilight or mist paints it with the shimmering blue of a Claude Monet, is the Palace of Westminster. That famous view from across the river, whence its great size (extending over eight acres) and its variegated silhouette can be appreciated, is substantially as it has been since the plans of Sir Charles Barry took material shape between 1840 and 1860 and in spite of attacks upon it. The species of limestone of which it is built has been susceptible to corrosive elements in the London air, the ornament devised by the Gothic enthusiast, Augustus Welby Northmore Pugin, has sadly crumbled (many a griffin, removed and sold, has become, at last, a garden ornament), for a long period the web of scaffolding that covered its towers added to its intricacy of line. Though there is a new interior House of Commons replacing the Chamber destroyed by a German bomb—in the new lobby, the "Churchill Arch" is a single battered survival from the ruins—externally change is imperceptible. If the view is always as strange in one way, as, in another familiar, it is because of the duality in the architect's thought that caused him to invest a plan of classic regularity with the imaginative features of a "Gothic" style that is somewhere between Perpendicular and Tudor and wholly of the nineteenth century.

It is a symbol of government that is something more or other than architecture; though one knows that every part has its necessary purpose. The long face of the "Gothic cliff" above the Terrace where Members and their friends take tea is a range of libraries and committee-rooms, the Speaker's Residence projecting at one end, the residences of Librarian and Black Rod at the other. The Victoria Tower, highest of all, 420 feet to the tip of its flagstaff, houses important documents, the Central Tower above the Central Hall (midway between the House of Commons and the House of Lords) contains the ventilating system, the Clock Tower gives us Big Ben and yet the visual fascination is apart, neither increased nor dispelled by informative analysis, that of a dream-like palace, mysterious still in its endless fretted detail, its turrets and pinnacles.

In contrast with this romantic colossus, the Tower of London, its square White Tower surmounted by gaily fluttering flag, has the crispness of a mediaeval illumination. It is, like the Abbey, a place commonly described in terms of its historical associations; of the fortress, the palace, the prison, that preceded the barracks and museum of today. Each of the thirteen towers of the inward ward has held its captives yet though one may reflect on its sombre record of suffering, execution and state necessity —not altogether as far away as the days of the Plantagenets and Tudors —here Roger Casement was executed in 1916 for his part in Irish rebellion, the "Officer in the Tower" and the Nazi, Rudolf Hess, incarcerated— nevertheless it is far from gloomy to look at: and if one thinks of the Kremlin as a comparable institution it takes on, in contrast, a homely charm. Partly this is due to its situation. Compactly self-contained within its dry moat and surrounding outer wall, it is remote from modern life and yet in a pleasant relation with it: with the traffic on the river; the Victorian warehouses to the west; the florid tower of Sir Edwin Cooper's Port of London Authority building with its uninhibited profusion of symbolic sculpture; the fantastic gateway of Tower Bridge; the wharf on which one can stroll among antique and captured cannon; the little beach where young Londoners bathe. To use once more the word "grey" is to leave out of account the "colour" implied by the stir and movement around it as well as the colour of the past, reticent in the bonnet and dark blue "undress" of the Yeomen of the Guard but exchanged for the Tudor reds and yellows of state occasions.

III Along the River

THE Thames is the magnificent sight it has always been; no less mysterious in those eastern reaches where from the vantage point of the "Prospect of Whitby", let us say, or, farther on, from the terrace of a tavern in the Isle of Dogs, it melts into a distant confusion of ships, cranes and warehouses, luring the imagination towards those still more mysterious reaches where it winds, by creeks, marshes and forgotten churches to the sea. It is as capable as ever of those surprises and riches of atmospheric colour that inspired Turner at Rotherhithe, Whistler at

Chelsea and Monet on the Embankment; at some points—and times—gentle, quiet and aloof—at others a bustling and crowded highway.

There are changes on its shores: the panorama of mouldering wharves and ruinous buildings on the South Bank, entrancing to the artist's eye, deplorable to that of the planner, has gone. From a room in the Savoy, the Austrian artist, Oscar Kokoschka, who used to paint the inchoate scene with affectionate abandon, has since viewed with less favour the clearance of the Festival year and the Royal Festival Hall in its cultural isolation. The dusky beast that surmounted the Lion Brewery, landmark of the old London, now appears, at close quarters, in startling magenta outside Waterloo Station. Large office buildings give their bluntness of silhouette to the skyline; from Westminster Bridge, looking towards St. Paul's, Shell-Mex House in the Strand prominent among them, they pile up like great sugar-cubes.

Even on the river there are changes. The red sails of the old barges have long ceased to be in evidence, the modernity of new buildings is matched by that of new ships, clean of line, immaculate of paint, among the seasoned cargo boats and smoky little tugs, yet in essentials the busy spectacle of the Pool of London, where the rattle of unloading blends with the roar of traffic, is unaltered and the Tower Bridge remains, if not a work of art, undoubtedly a wonder. It is also, like other of the larger undertakings of the Gothically-minded nineteenth century, a fascinating contradiction which the passage of time has not in any way lessened. A dream of the past are these towers—a repetition by Sir Wolfe Barry of the towers of Westminster conceived by his father, Sir Charles—yet we know that they are, in fact, constructed of steel, that the thousand tons of each half of the roadway can be raised to let ships through, by hydraulic machinery, in a minute and a half. Realism and romance go together; archaism and science; the stylistic nostalgia is offset by the complete confidence of the feat of engineering—mercifully, the tinted mists of the river give their own poetry to both. No generalisation will suffice for the majestic sweep of the Thames from, let us say, Chiswick to Millwall. We are thrown back on the "minute particulars" (to use William Blake's phrase). It is one thing to look out across its waters from some narrow alley, or landing stage where the tall wooden piles provide a faintly Venetian foreground for the warehouses and docks: another, to see it, from the series of embankments, extending between Blackfriars Bridge and Chelsea. Coming away from the murky industrial magnificence of the eastward Thames (though still within the industrial zone) let us pause for contrast on the embankment of Chelsea Reach. A touch of welcome green on the opposite shore is Battersea Park, patches of brighter riverside colour locate the Pleasure Gardens, and there among gracious trees, is that historic row of houses, Cheyne Walk, completion and extension of a riverside village, beautiful, and spotless from the respectful care the twentieth century has accorded to the eighteenth.

IV Squares and Open Places

HOW varied are the squares and open places. Movement and colour combine to make Piccadilly Circus a day- and night-long excitement. The traffic that careers endlessly round it, to and from Piccadilly, Regent Street, Shaftesbury Avenue and Leicester Square, intermingled with the crowds of pedestrians, is a moving mosaic, dominated by the red of the London buses. If you wait long enough here, it is said, you will in due time see everyone you know; it is certainly true you will see every kind of automobile, elderly survivals, pertly bright sports cars, showily magnificent limousines, the aristocratic refinement of the Rolls. Piccadilly Circus is not grey—all is warmth; on the sunny buff wall of the Pavilion corner, even in daytime, the advertising signs are a vivid pattern —an alternative scheme to the neon brilliance of night. There are flower-sellers still, though not so many as there used to be, on the steps of the Shaftesbury Memorial Fountain, their baskets of blooms standing out against its coppery-green. The fountain has all its old suggestion of the nineties, not only in its association with boat race nights but in its style, the "art nouveau" of that period which its designer, Sir Alfred Gilbert, turned to such masterly account. Eros as gracefully as ever shoots his aluminium arrow (though naughtily, since his reinstallation, away from the avenue named after the benevolent Earl of Shaftesbury—to which it was once the archer's function to direct our notice). The façade of the Criterion has its memory of Edwardian pleasures. Here is the square of tradition but with a dense, rich texture of modern life.

As much may be said of Trafalgar Square. By no outward sign does the National Gallery reveal that loss of space caused by bombing, only gradually reclaimed. The scene it overlooks has its familiar cool grandeur —the lions of Sir Edwin Landseer in their darkened bronze at the foot of Nelson's granite column look amiably towards the superb steeple and Corinthian portico of James Gibbs's masterpiece, St. Martin-in-the-Fields; towards South Africa House, with its gilt springbok, and the refashioned classicism of Canada House. It looks its best in summer when, from the porch of the National Gallery, amateur photographers of many nations train their cameras on Whitehall, when the fountains, in which the con-temporary sculptor's tritons twist and turn, send their spray drifting over a cosmopolitan crowd—blond, peaked-capped students from Scandinavia,

16

Orientals in richness of turban and robe, and all the strollers, native Londoners, provincials, foreigners, who stop to feed and admire the tamest and haughtiest pigeons in the world. In contrast Leicester Square is not what it was—one thinks with regret of the almost rural seclusion of its gardens as they were within living memory, of the crescents on the gilt domes of the departed Alhambra, the busts of its local great men: Hogarth and Reynolds, Hunter and Newton, ranged in silent homage round the central figure of Shakespeare—but seclusion is gone. Cinemaland, a much-trodden open space, it has yielded to the pressures of change and war.

Whether a square should be open or not is a delicate question. We shall never see again, probably, those miles of iron spears that surrounded every town patch of green. Parliament Square freed of Victorian iron-work (of especially curious pattern), its statuary disposed in orderly fashion and plainer view represents a modern impatience with exclusion. Yet there is an individual character in the gardens of the great squares that needs to be preserved. Consider the abundant plantations of the most distinguished of them, the late eighteenth-century Bedford Square, or the ambitious layout of Grosvenor Square, the gardens of which were originally designed by Kent for Sir Richard Grosvenor.

Grosvenor Square, without that sober completeness and dignity of proportion that characterise Bedford and St. James's, retains the air of wealth and luxury, the successive layers of grandeur of the eighteenth, nineteenth and twentieth centuries. It takes us back to the days when the torches of the link-men lit up the arrival of fashionable Georgian guests, then to the opulent zenith of the Victorian age when Jeames Yellowplush admitted the crinolined ladies to the brick mansions (by that time faced with more splendid stone) and now, the American Embassy is its architectural keynote—it is since the war especially a square of American memories and incident—from Sir Reid Dick's statue of President Roosevelt, to the vast, sleek, automobiles that enliven it with their transatlantic colour. Equally with an air of splendour, though more consistently of the nineteenth century is Belgrave Square, long its rival in fashion and displaying that array of columned porches which became the hall-mark of Victorian pride.

V West End

"BELGRAVIA" is the southern extremity of the West End— and what is the West End? To say that it is an area bounded by Charing Cross on the one hand and Hyde Park on the other is dull and unexplanatory. One must select some metropolitan pleasure to accompany and interpret it. It is, to some extent, the routine of the person of fashion. Even now when everyone works and it is vaguely reprehensible to loiter, the mid-morning pace, in Piccadilly, as the Circus is left behind, slackens, the fewer figures on the pavement seem to wear clothes of unusual quality and chic. They stroll, which the Londoner's active conscience normally does not permit. They linger over the richly tooled bindings of rare editions in a window of Hatchard's, or exotic sweetmeats in a window of Fortnum and Mason's or ponder the French Travel Agency's gastronomic map of France. They turn to go along the Burlington Arcade, that feast of small finery, toys and trinkets, of fancy waistcoats and old school ties, of curious sets of carved chessmen, of expensive bracelets. Sooner or later they will come into Bond Street, of which except in terms of further fascinating shop windows it is difficult to give any adequate description in words. Narrow, confused, it has no feature so definite as the swaggering quadrant of Regent Street—nor the latter's spaciousness—and yet an atmosphere of—the old-fashioned word is essential—elegance. There is little temptation to lift the eyes above window level—unless to gaze at the abstract sculptured frieze by Henry Moore on the *Time* and *Life* building—that modern packing case among the unobtrusive and decorous fronts. Its colour is accessory yet how varied—from the French Impressionist in one of its art dealers' shops to the finest of hand-woven tweeds.

Mayfair, hard by, has changed rather in nature than appearance—Curzon Street and Hertford Street are streets of stately houses still, but commerce has crept in—though with a sympathetic refinement—small and well-lettered nameplates, on close examination, will reveal that many a former mansion is now the headquarters of an industrial corporation or an advertising agency. It is round the corner, in the stables and garages that fashion makes its domestic stand, in the "cottage with a double coach house, a cottage of gentility": in these bypaths that colour blooms in window boxes and on bright front doors. So potent is a name that there is still a suggestion of Watteau pastoral in this land of a bygone May Fair, though Shepherd's Market on its site, has nothing to do with shepherds and shepherdesses in this idyllic context, was once quite prosaically the property of a Mr. Shepherd. Yet, approached through an archway from Curzon Street, or by a narrow alley from Piccadilly, it is fascinating as one of those village-like oases which are everywhere embedded in London, though with its own individual mixture of the smart and the popular. The butcher's, the fishmonger's, the old-fashioned public house are complemented by the antique shops with their fragile chairs, glass lustres, and old cottage ornaments. The little café-eating-houses where advertising executives discuss their accounts over the coffee-cups; cafés, Italian only in a pleasantly cockney sense, have their more consciously continental neighbour, with a striped awning, and, greatly daring, tables and chairs outside beneath it. The exclusive dinner club, the utilitarian sandwich-bar, these are contrasts that give their spice and picturesqueness.

The West End is a flavour; of art, of entertainment, of wealth, and, in its club zone, of seclusive dignity. St. James's Street, looking almost exactly like the street depicted by Hogarth in *The Rake's Progress* with the distinctive mellow brick of St. James's Palace at the end, still invites us to admire its famous club façades, the bow-window of White's (James Wyatt, 1776). Boodle's with its row of medallions (Robert Adam, 1775), Brooks's (Henry Holland, 1777). The clubs give their classic seclusion to Pall Mall—the Athenæum shines out at the corner of Waterloo Place in the refurbished splendour of 1830 that recalls the devotion of that period to Greece; the effect of the frieze copied from the Parthenon heightened by a ground of blue; the statue of Pallas Athene (by Edward Hodges Baily) flashing with gold.

Alternatively one may view the West End as a region fringed and seamed with parks, more welcome as the tide of twentieth-century traffic gains impetus. St. James's Park, Green Park, Hyde Park—it is still a remarkable thought that, allowing for one or two crossings one can walk all the way from Whitehall to Kensington Palace among trees, flower beds and stretches of green. St. James's Park is a delicate miniature, leading the eye to Buckingham Palace, Green Park a rural pasture that brings us to the tumult of Hyde Park Corner. Hyde Park is gay with its Lido, its open-air restaurant and the present-day Park Lane on its eastern side, changed out of all recognition from the bow-fronted, balconied "million-aire's row" it is possible to remember; the red and buff promontories of Grosvenor House and the Dorchester rising above the red buses, Oxford Street or Piccadilly bound, looking over the populous inner road of the Park and aglow with modernity.

VI Central London

CENTRAL London is full of surprises. Leave Regent Street, by one of those few passages on its eastern side that the architect John Nash grudgingly allowed when he sealed off a "vulgar" quarter and opened a fair, new prospect to the West; and you enter a separate, inner city, full of secret and devious ways. Turn off the Strand and you may light on some ancient court in which a "pocket" of Dickensian domestic life persists as if, because tucked out of sight, it had been forgotten by the world. The Strand itself, from which one can hardly separate its many interesting bypaths, is full of surprises, a whole series of contrasts which, as with Bond Street, makes it easier to say what is in it than what it looks like. There are the two exquisite churches on their island sites, exquisite, though they have remained ruinous since the war: St. Clement Danes, the beautiful Wren church to which Gibbs added a graceful spire—Dr. Johnson, as sculptured by Percy Fitzgerald, still pores over his book outside the shattered east end; and St. Mary-le-Strand, another of the splendid conceptions of James Gibbs, belonging to the reign of Queen Anne. The eighteenth-century element is reinforced by the grey Georgian magnificence of Sir William Chambers's Somerset House and its east wing (King's College) added by Soane's pupil, Sir Robert Smirke (pictorially, to look away from the Strand, by Somerset House towards Waterloo Bridge is like finding an old master and a modern "primitive" in juxtaposition). Yet the Strand begins and ends with nineteenth-century Gothic, for so Eleanor's Cross in the courtyard of Charing Cross Station must be called (even though it copies a mediaeval original) and so of course is the last great secular experiment in the ancient style, George Street's Royal Courts of Justice, massive and even simple in spite of pinnacles and arcades. All the large buildings of the Strand, while not exactly unneighbourly, are absorbed in themselves and their special purposes, they conform to no architectural plan other than their own— the Savoy Hotel, the Strand Palace Hotel, Shell-Mex House, Australia House and India House. The two latter, flanking Harvey Corbett's Bush House (which is less of the Strand than an American peroration to Kings-way) have their individuality distinct from it and from that of each other.

Yet this is not the whole of the Strand—it is dotted with little shops, some—perpetually at the moment of "Final Clearance"—gaudy with check shirts and lumber-jackets of purple and emerald green, some chock-a-block with "left luggage", their trunks and umbrellas spilling on the pavement. It is lined with parentheses, here a dark entry that leads to a Roman bath; Robert Street, that takes us into the Adelphi, or what is left of it; byways that lead to Covent Garden Market, others that bring us into the calm precincts of the Temple. The Strand, altogether, is hand-some and mean, commonplace and studded with beauties, carelessly trailing history round its skirts, the strangest combination of new and old.

Fleet Street is dominated and disciplined, architecturally by St. Paul's, though it has the same happy-go-lucky colour and incident that one finds elsewhere. An American journalist was once shocked by posters on the walls adjoining the Ludgate Circus railway viaduct—in his native Balti-more, he explained, it would have been considered vandalism requiring some sharp rebuke or penalty thus to disfigure a venerable scene—but in London, as in this instance, everything is incorporated into the visual effect. The green-painted iron railway bridge of what was once the South-Eastern and Chatham Railway would formerly to some fastidious eyes have been vandalism in itself, yet it has grown into a familiar and tolerable relation with the great dome, the glimpses of St. Paul's façade, the little steeple of St. Martin Ludgate, by Wren (1684), that so entertainingly obstructs the view of the greater church; and the bridge becomes relatively a quaint survival in contrast with the black glass and stainless steel of the *Daily Express* building at Shoe Lane. Dr. Johnson would not have known this Fleet Street; save in such fragments as the restored seventeenth-century house, opposite Chancery Lane, that contains "Prince Henry's Room"; the clock with the wooden giants that strike the hours, of St. Dunstan's in the West (though the church itself is rebuilt) or the hostelry he and Boswell frequented, richly brown in its ancient woodwork, the "Cheshire Cheese", or the little Courts leading to the familiar spectacle of his house in Gough Square. He would have stared with surprise at the Griffin of 1880 by Charles Bell Birch, replacing Temple Bar, at the black-and-white of that modern innovation, the milk bar, no less at the frontage that speaks always of News—and the unquiet byways where the hum of the printing presses grows louder.

VII The City

THE City is Victorian darkness, tempered by the gleam of modern offices and banks, and the open spaces left over from war-time devastation. In spite of the latter, what an intricacy and vastness remains. Those dingy fronts, on which the sculptured, bearded heads of a Victorian mythology glare in blackened stone, those porches where the clustered brass plates bearing the names of enterprises that stretch all over the world are polished to an antique fineness. The imagination penetrates into boardrooms sombre with mahogany and horse-hair, shabby centres of trade and industry that encircle the globe. The ancient city of Romans and Saxons lies underground, leaving a surface track, mainly of names, its boundaries indicated by "London Wall" and by the vanished gates—Ludgate, Newgate, Bishopsgate, Moorgate, Aldgate. The brook that flowed through the centre of this nucleus city is a sewer; yet the chance archaeology of bombing and rebuilding has made its slight additions to what one can see—fresh fragments of Roman wall and in 1954 the Mithraic temple that stood once on the Wallbrook bank, a discovery that drew thousands of fascinated Londoners and is now saved from resepulture: while the finds of late years have added handsomely to the collection of the Guildhall Museum: from a pin or a bottle to the coarse blubber-mouthed features of a provincial Roman carved perhaps by a native sculptor.

Guildhall, Council Hall of the City, is a building that stirs the sense of the past more by its associations than its external splendour. It stands in modest, grey seclusion in its courtyard, as one approaches from Cheapside by King Street. The front, designed by George Dance in 1789, is, to the modern eye, a not unpleasing interpretation of Gothic, though the fact that it is an interpretation recalls the chequered history of a structure frequently renewed. Built in the early fifteenth century on the site of an earlier administrative centre, partly burnt down in the Great Fire, refronted by Dance, restored and remodelled internally by Sir Horace Jones, between 1864 and 1870, it was again severely damaged by fire in 1940 when the roof of the Great Hall was completely destroyed. "A mean-looking Hôtel de Ville", the comment of a Victorian critic on its exterior has just sufficient point to make it resented by all those proud of the Guildhall's ancient lustre—though the comment was a criticism of the Gothic of 1789 and implied a wish for the greater sumptuousness of Victorian revival which not all would now share. Yet the basically noble proportions of the Great Hall, 152 feet long, 50 feet broad, 89 feet high, remain in the interior, once again restored, with stone arches and a flat panelled ceiling, by Sir Giles Scott (1954). Colour is in the mind's eye, in the memory of state occasions, banquets, pageants, of which the paintings in the Guildhall Art Gallery have also their visual reminder.

Seeking a focus of this extraordinary warren of commerce, the City, built so pertinaciously on the ground plan of the narrow, crooked streets and alleys of the Middle Ages, one comes to the Bank, the Mansion House and the Royal Exchange. Here that ever-hurrying crowd, distinguished from other London crowds by the bowlers, the top-hats of bank messengers, the umbrellas, and dark clothes that add their subfusc detail to the City's solemnity, reaches its maximum congestion, surges in the morning up the long treads of the Mansion House Underground Station, of "the Bank", darts this way and that among the roaring vermilion buses, along Poultry, Cornhill, Threadneedle Street and narrow Lombard Street—and in the evening is magically gone down its tubes, leaving no trace behind. The Bank is as remarkable as any of the numerous London buildings in which some aspiration or thought, or, alternatively, some not strictly architectural process of organic growth, causes us to look on it with the wonder that attaches to life rather than to art. Not one building but two, it is a kind of economic evolution in itself; the complexity of a vast modern financial organisation bursting through the established limits of an earlier age. It is curious to think that it should originally have been of one story, as indicated by the windowless façade, adapted by Sir John Soane in the nicety of classic revival (1795–1827) from the Augustan Temple of Vesta at Tivoli. Within this bastion of tradition rises the glittering new building designed by Sir Herbert Baker with its grandiose colonnade, with the sculptured figures by Charles Wheeler, in symbolic alignment (his Ariel on the dome is an "Eros" of finance), and on the pediment, the "Lady of Threadneedle Street", not that old "White Lady of Threadneedle Street", who once pathetically haunted the Bank, but the allegory of a newer tradition, with fluttering robes and the model of the old building on her knee.

In contrast with the Bank the Royal Exchange, which seems to lack any certain modern function save that of a gallery and is now to house exhibits from the Guildhall Museum, stands with somewhat lonely and shadowy dignity, withdrawing a little from the busy crowds and looking older than its age, for its grimy Corinthian portico dates only from 1842 when Sir William Tite designed the third building to stand on this site. The City is a vast field for the connoisseur of British sculpture in its lesser-known manifestations, among which is the group in the tympanum of the Exchange by Richard Westmacott—where Commerce extends her welcome equally to the British merchant, the Arab, Indian and Turk. It is complemented by Sir Robert Taylor's allegorical group over the Mansion House—in which London, partnered by Plenty, triumphs over envious rivalry. Older than the Royal Exchange, though also with its Corinthian portico, designed by George Dance the elder in 1739, the Mansion House surpasses it in impressiveness and its dignity as the official residence of the Lord Mayor, and his great banqueting hall.

To examine the curious details of City architecture and sculpture it is necessary to go of a week-end when that wonderfully dramatic transformation has taken place, the tide of life has completely gone out, and what is left is a kind of overgrown Pompeii, a dead place yet exactly as when its inhabitants quitted it. On a Sunday one can savour the past at leisure in the names of its thoroughfares, from Milk Street to Crutched Friars; lose oneself in a maze of deserted alleys and courts, linger over the beautiful remnants of the City churches, study the forest of modern commercial signs in Lombard Street, and wander undisturbed among the closed warehouses by the river with their Piranesi-like galleries. Most dramatic of all is it to press on eastwards beyond the Aldgate Pump, when the world comes to life again, the sound of people talking comes strangely after the prolonged silence, there are shops open and stalls in the street—the colour of the East End replaces the City's sombre aspect.

VIII Eastward London

HAS the East End colour? The grim wood-engravings of Gustave Doré's London leave impressed upon the mind a vision of endless mysterious and darkling streets, depth upon depth of darkness, parallel with the mystery of the eastward Thames. Some, though not all, of this mystery has gone. Isolated and decayed little dockland villages (like Leamouth) were swept away by the London County Council before 1939. There is little of Oriental colour now in Limehouse. The rain of 15,000 bombs that fell on this part of London made its clearance. Poplar is the chosen ground of model reconstruction—in "Lansbury", between the Limehouse Cut and the East India Dock Road—on idealistic modern lines. What East London, on either bank, reveals depends where you go; if as far as Greenwich it will be to find Blackheath in these days once more as spruce and fashionably domestic as at the beginning of the nineteenth century. In between there are still stretches of those little houses of darkened buff over whose rusty chimneys rise the white and red funnels, the orange masts of the big ships in the dock basins; there are beautiful, ancient houses marooned amid squalor—yet to seek out and disentangle the present state of east London is an exploration beyond our present scope. Certainly Whitechapel has its own liveliness of colour and Middlesex Street on Sunday morning, to go no farther, halting at the meeting point of east and west, is as colourful a market as it used to be in its earlier guise and description as "Petticoat Lane".

* * *

One pauses to think of London's markets in general, of Smithfield, Billingsgate, Covent Garden—the latter as a spectacle must ever be a favourite of the visitor not only for its flowers and fruit but for the persistence of the historic elements in its décor, the weighty porch of St. Paul's (originally Inigo Jones's) with King Street behind, looking now exactly as in Hogarth's *Times of Day*—and in many an early English water-colour —the porters balancing their baskets seem of an historic cockney type. To turn from the necessities to the rarer pleasures of life is to think also of Christie's auction rooms, restored to their old home in King Street, St. James's, or of entering Sotheby's through its quaintly Gothic, Bond Street porch; in either gallery to watch the marketing of the art of the world—from a Canaletto to a Picasso. . . .

* * *

But Middlesex Street is of lower degree—as the old name "Petticoat Lane" suggests, once a market of old clothes, to be compared with the vanished "Rag Fair" of Rosemary Lane (or Mint Street) so vividly pictured

24

by Rowlandson. Clothing is still a main item in Whitechapel's trade, as the modernistic shop fronts of Middlesex Street (defying its sooty brick) announce, but it is the most miscellaneous of fairs that is held there of a Sunday, decorative rather than useful, a show for the general entertainment, attended by London's most closely-packed crowd. Sightseers from all quarters and natives of the district move at the slowest of paces past the stalls where the red-faced hucksters roar out their patter.

Mysterious elixirs are deeply crimson in glass vessels. Alsatians in plaster gilt, vases of astounding design are held on high, praised with a raucous virtuosity of salesmanship. The polished brass tripod with its seat of red plush invites you to try your weight; the white-coated pedlar of hair restorer runs fingers persuasively through the locks of a waxen head, men of roguish expression carry fleets of bright balloons, and elicit squeaks from gaudy toys. Here is a place to study both popular life—and popular art.

IX Colour Ceremonial

ONE cannot speak of the colour of London without mention of its pageantry and ceremony, royal, military, heraldic. It is a tradition productive of effects strangely at variance with the more or less uniform aspect of an equalitarian democracy—though on that account all the more striking. Whitehall would not be Whitehall without the mounted sentries at the building known as the Horse Guards, so called because a troop of the cavalry, originally formed by Charles II, is always on duty there. Strange survival indeed in the days of drab khaki and mechanised warfare but how brilliantly effective the white plume, gauntlets and buckskin breeches, the polished top-boots of antique cut, the flashing helmet, breastplate and sword, investing the motionless figure on his horse with heroic splendour. Or in the forecourt of Buckingham Palace, behind the railings tipped with their golden fleurs-de-lis, at half-past ten in the morning there is the brave sight of the Changing of the Guard—the colour scheme of red tunic, blue trousers and bearskin set in movement of exact precision. Or in the evening, at some point on their route from Wellington Barracks you may encounter the detachment of Guards (again in their bearskins, and with long grey coats) that marches to take up its time-honoured duty of guarding the vaults of the Bank of England.

A portrait of London is not complete without these notes of decided colour that are a feature of its everyday routine aspect. From this the greater ceremonies must be considered apart. It is only once a year that the fairy-tale coach of the Lord Mayor, with its gorgeously attired coachmen, is seen in the Lord Mayor's Show, together with the motor-drawn floats with their modern allegories and displays—such as "The Navy Spans the World". It is not in quite the same category as the daily pageantry of the city, which to so many visitors seems the essential London. It would, however, evidently be a mistake to think of this as merely a metropolitan attraction. One might almost call it functional—here colour represents or is interwoven with the sense of history, esprit de corps, the pride of tradition.

X The Old and New London

IT is with a revived or sharpened sense of period that one looks, or may with advantage look at the London of today. There is so much that we have learnt to appreciate only by degrees even though extreme age or exceptional beauty have never lacked appreciation. Westminster Abbey or Westminster Hall (with its wonderful hammer-beamed roof) could command the respect even of an Augustan age, little disposed on the whole to admire "Gothick"; but the nineteenth century, reversing prejudice, was not very tolerant of any of the City's classic additions from the seventeenth century onwards: William Morris, by no means alone in his view, thought St. Paul's ugly: all the architecture of Queen Anne was in his time dismissed as dull or, at best, quaint. The ordered planning of the Georgian architects in Tennyson's eyes, for instance, was "unlovely". "Queen Anne" began to be readmired in the late nineteenth century when such an architect as Norman Shaw paid it the compliment of (free) imitation. Georgian buildings have not, until our own century, been treated with any marked regard—it was their wholesale destruction in the nineteen-twenties that rallied the Georgian Group to defence. London possesses such a plenty of the smaller Georgian houses that familiarity has bred indifference, though this the post-war building famine has done much to dispel. The process of reassessment has gone further: appreciation has ventured into the curious territory of nineteenth-century "revival"—full certainly of interest and even excitement—as well as imperfections—among which may be counted the yearning for colour expressed in material often unsympathetic to the London climate. An unyielding, an unweathering element gives its harshness to the terra-cotta surface of Waterhouse's Natural History Museum, South Kensington, the Ross of Mull granite of the Albert Memorial's columns, its Salviati mosaic which time can neither mellow or corrode.

The polychrome London of the nineteenth-century architects is a special study: needing to be remarked on here as adding to the depth of present-day perspective. Each successive stage reached by appreciation, by contrast or otherwise, brings into clearer view the achievements of the past, and makes not only a few famous buildings but every London street a delight to "discover".

What superb dignity of proportion there is for instance in Queen Anne's Gate, originally known as Queen's Square and laid out in the admirable fashion of the early eighteenth century, as a whole. The feeling of the past, the sense of "period" is particularly strong—nothing incongruous (in spite of some alterations) disturbs it as you enter its quietude from Birdcage Walk. The period feeling is increased by the charming small statue of Queen Anne, in brocaded skirt and bodice and with orb and sceptre on her railed-in pedestal by No. 15. The bands of stone marking the floor levels are a spacious design in themselves, the mellow bricks even seem to have been made and lovingly placed in position by an artist; the keystones above the ground- and first-floor windows are carved with excellent grotesque masks (with what symbolic satyr-life Dickens would have invested them!), the entrance doorways with their graceful fanlights and carved hoods are the most impressive of departures from the general restraint. Nowadays we do not often use the word "noble", yet this seems the fitting description for the architecture of Queen Anne's Gate.

It is perhaps (regarded as a unity) more palatial than that other famous group of buildings, Kensington Palace, belonging substantially to the same era, though part of it is somewhat earlier, the new buildings added to and replacing the original "Nottingham House" being designed for William III by Sir Christopher Wren, and much alteration and rebuilding carried out for George I by that talented designer of décors, William Kent. The beautifully proportioned Orangery by Wren belongs to the same year as Queen Anne's Gate. Here restraint becomes distinct understatement— never has royalty lived in a less grandiose setting. The Palace is not lofty, it is almost entirely devoid of external ornament; by comparison with the splendour of Versailles it seems humble indeed. On the other hand one may reflect that Versailles has at last become a brilliant monstrosity, the surprising husk of an entirely obsolete political order. Kensington Palace —ever so quietly—asserts the greater dignity of an absence of ostentation, the permanence of simplicity.

Perhaps one sees it best on an autumn day, when red brick and green slates take on a warm glow against the yellow and russets of the trees in the Gardens. It looks domestic and mild (though in traditional English fashion the interior is less restrained—in its balustrades, cornices, panelling and stately proportion). A royal residence once more, this house where Queen Victoria was born, and as a girl received news of her accession, is an engaging product of the national character.

Dignity, restraint, calm, the effect of a cloister in the bustle of London, these are the virtues, soothing to the spirit, of late seventeenth- and eighteenth-century planning; to be found concentrated in the Inns of Court; in the Temple, and Gray's Inn, sadly damaged and much reconstructed as they have been; merged with impressive result in the façades of New Square, Lincoln's Inn. A walk through Holborn (as a borough) is a progress through a remarkable phase of town design. As in the Inns of Court, one recognises the same genius of style in the houses of Great Ormond Street, at the beginning of the eighteenth century, expanding into the eventual magnificence of Bedford Square, about 1775. But the eighteenth century is still everywhere in London, in greater or lesser consistence, from east to west, from north to south, tempering it with sobriety and order, a recurring warm and humane note in its varied colour scheme.

There follows it that engulfing wave, the onrush of Victorian expansion, in which, dazzled by the confusion and multitude of architectural images, the eye turns to the skyline and finds the aesthetic aspirations of the period perhaps most completely expressed in the silhouette, linear and intricate, adapted to a somewhat misty condition of atmosphere. Wren had not been unappreciative of the mediaeval legacy of steeple and spire though the full symphonic effect of the City churches, as a pattern of tapering shafts, is now lost from view; but the Gothic Revivalist, Sir George Gilbert Scott, wished to restore more completely the mediaeval skyline, attempted it in St. Pancras Station, using all his knowledge of French and Venetian Gothic—equally with the Houses of Parliament and Tower Bridge it displays a fantasy of outline that is curiously fascinating when a golden sky paints a dim purple-blue its gables and dormers, its turrets and towers.

The pace of change in the twentieth century has quickened—the "Battle of the Styles" in which the Gothic enthusiasts were finally routed, has changed ground and character—as far as it persists it lies between the negation of all past styles, the modern insistence on the plainest and most direct solution of an architectural problem; and the lingering protest against uniformity and regularity, the feeling that the majesty and importance of great buildings in the capital needs to be assured by the classic column, the rounded arch. From fourth floor to cornice, the huge Ionic colonnade of Unilever House, administrative centre of all Port Sunlight's industries, gleams whitely above the eighteen-sixtyish granite and iron of Cubitt's Blackfriars Bridge. The column and arch of "English Renaissance" play their part in variegating the vast surfaces of Thames House and Imperial Chemical House on Millbank—industrial walls enclosing Sir Edwin Lutyens' more domestic and intimate conception of a new Westminster.

In contrast other modern buildings reject "style" and gain individual interest by their adaptation to function and site—the series of blocks composing 55, Broadway, Headquarters of London's Underground, is one example—another is Val Myer's Broadcasting House, outer shell of the honeycomb of studios and offices, so skilfully making the best of an awkward corner and rising in its oval simplicity, rather like the hull of a great ship, above its surroundings.

On this modern architecture, the sculpture in which London has always been prolific has a hold still, though it becomes increasingly tenuous. With its own allowance of architectural space, Edwardian sculpture has a florid confidence. Sir Bertram Mackennal's chariot of the sun rides proudly above the entrance to Australia House, the figures of Youth under the arch of the Kingsway front of Bush House are a necessary and central feature of its design, Selfridge's clock is a riot of sculpture—but later the allotment is more spartan. Epstein's figures of Night and Day at the Underground's offices encroach upon austerity, so, too, does Eric Gill's Prospero over the doorway of Broadcasting House. The figure of Architecture is an isolated relief on the severe rectangular front of the Royal Institute of British Architects building. Last of all comes the type of structure so purely abstract or purposeful in design that ornament of any kind is inadmissible. It would spoil the sweeping curve of Peter Jones's store at Sloane Square, it would be manifestly out of place in the handsome rotunda of flats that opposes its modernity to the columned porches of Belgrave Square or·on the cubic balconies of the flats at Highpoint, Highgate.

What is the effect of all these developments on the eye, on the total aspect and colour of London? Can we imagine its dusky massiveness exchanged for immaculate stretches of white wall, with windows punched in to a uniform pattern? This is the change that some individual buildings project, suggesting sometimes a city of immature skyscrapers, sometimes the delight in new forms and materials that seems fitting to a "machine age". The contrast with the old London can be startling—but so have been many previous contrasts in the course of its history. It is the greatness of London to renew itself constantly—it is a living organism that is never complete, nor at the same time capable of entire transformation. The "genius of the place" is that of an abundant and even careless-seeming variety—perfection of plan has not been in its nature. Planning has been time after time lost in its complexity—the magnificence of Kingsway becomes indecisive, Cromwell Road after an ambitious start tails away, the terraces of Nash remain the grandiose fragments of an unfinished scheme, Wren's plan never got beyond paper. On the other hand how much of its historical self it has preserved and kept alive; and into what splendid and diversified pictures it is resolved, the colour photograph makes us freshly aware. Brick, stucco and Portland stone, London; classic, Gothic, modern; the London of park and river; here is the "Flower of Cities all" tinted with the hues of reality.

Index

Regent's Park

Regent's Park is the most countrified of London's parks but its 450 acres allow for a great deal of variety and a number of diversions, from the Zoological Gardens on its northern perimeter, to the boating lake at the south, seen in our photograph; and it is not merely an enclosed piece of country but an area ambitiously planned. Laid out by John Nash in 1812, it involved the destruction of many straggling farms and cottages on the old "Marylebone Park Fields" though ancient trees were preserved, and it was not complete until 1838. Roughly circular, bounded to the north by the curve of the Regent's Canal, it was intended as a sumptuous "garden city", rimmed with stately terraces, studded with the villas of the wealthy and with a palace—for the Prince Regent—at its centre (or, rather, Inner Circle). The palace remained a project, the Inner Circle since 1932 has given to the public the Open Air Theatre, but terraces, some villas and the ornamental water are existing parts of the original grand design. The Holme on the shores of the lake, designed by Decimus Burton about 1818 for his father, a rich builder, and having a Corinthian portico, is one of the southern landmarks—like a country house in its own quiet park—though South Villa not far away has been replaced by Bedford College. With its several islands, covered with trees and a tangle of shrubbery, the ornamental water somewhat resembles that of St. James's Park though it is on a larger scale. It rivals St. James's in the number and rare kinds of its water-birds (the flying bomb which fell in the lake during World War II killed some of them) but the bays and islands normally form ideal nesting-places). A walk round the banks and three armlets of water is still, in the words of *London and Its Vicinity Exhibited* (1851) "a most agreeable and picturesque promenade".

Clarence Terrace, Regent's Park

"Regent's Park and its circumjacent buildings promise, in a few years, to afford something like an equipoise to the boasted *Palace Group* of Paris . . . a union of rural and architectural beauty on a scale of greater magnificence than can be found in any other place," said a writer in Brande's *Quarterly Journal* in 1827; and the system of terraces, planned by John Nash, still justifies enthusiastic praise. They form a handsome rim to the southern sector of the Park's Outer Circle, and though varying to some extent in individual design, they have the same main features, a portico with pediment and wings, given a mansion-like dignity by columns of the Doric or Corinthian orders. The effect indeed is that of a single mansion (Regent's Park representing its grounds). In furtherance of this object and to give a unity of composition, what the *Quarterly Journal* called "the deformity of *door cases*" was for the most part avoided, and entrances made behind. Mansion-like dignity was further suggested by names mainly connected with royalty—Hanover Terrace, Cornwall Terrace, Clarence Terrace and so on. Chester Terrace, Cumberland Terrace and Hanover Terrace are in several respects the most imposing externally—in length, setting, or sculptural detail, but Clarence Terrace at the south-west is a most attractive example. with its bold projections and its Corinthian columns and pilasters. There is a sunny sparkle in the stucco freshly restored. The Regent's Park Terraces have been criticised for shoddiness of construction (blast during World War II exposed the flimsiness of some partition walls) but they remain a remarkable piece of architectural design.

Marble Arch

One looks down on a majestic scene at the north-east corner of Hyde Park, the white façades of cinema and hotel rising above the Marble Arch and repeating its Corinthian columns along their frontage, while the traffic to and from Oxford Street, Park Lane and Edgware Road circles on its round. Tyburn Tree, the gallows whither criminals (until 1783) were brought from Newgate to be hanged, which once stood, to the left at the angle of Connaught Place, is the faintest of squalid memories belonging to another world than this. The famous arch, designed by John Nash for George IV, was originally an approach to Buckingham Palace, but was moved to its present position in the year of the Great Exhibition, 1851. It was to have carried an equestrian statue of George IV by Sir Francis Chantrey and was first intended to commemorate the victories of Trafalgar and Waterloo but the reliefs, on the north by Westmacott and on the south by Baily, have a more general and pacific character. Solely ornamental, it now stands on an island, the railings of Hyde Park having been set back in 1908 to allow room for increasing traffic. It adds dignity and a name to this part of London (the marble of which it is built came from the quarries of Carrara) and that severe critic of metropolitan architecture, Augustus Hare, somewhat unfairly, called it "one of our national follies, a despicable caricature of the Arch of Constantine". The bronze gates, ornamented with scroll work, lions and the figure of St. George and the Dragon, designed and cast by Samuel Parker "of Argyll Street", are excellent in craftsmanship. The trees at the left in the photograph are a reminder that only a few yards behind them is the Park's "orators' corner" where the right of free speech is still exercised by soapbox speakers to the entertainment of the public.

The Round Pond

London seems far away from this sparkling stretch of bird-haunted water, yet the Round Pond is in no more rural surroundings than Kensington Gardens, equidistant between the Bayswater Road and High Street, Kensington, and in planned relation to Kensington Palace. It formed part of the layout made by the eighteenth-century garden architect, Bridgeman, for Queen Caroline, wife of George II, though the basin he designed is not exactly round but octagonal in shape (the word "pond", too, seems not altogether to suit a stretch of water seven acres in extent). It formed a central point from which long vistas stretched away—as far as the companion waters of the Serpentine—in one of the avenues between the two, the bronze cast of G. F. Watts's horse and rider —"Physical Energy"—is impressively placed.

The figures in the background remind us, however, that the Round Pond is not to be adequately described except in human terms. It is, as the rest of Kensington Gardens has been since the childhood days of Queen Victoria, a favoured resort of children—and of those in whom something of the child lingers. To sail model ships on its surface is an old established pastime—one imagines Shelley pushing out his paper boats and absorbed in watching how they fared. The young of all ages launch their yachts on its placid breadth—on a bright day with a breath of wind to fill the small sails the scene becomes lively as Cowes, the Round Pond takes on the air of regatta.

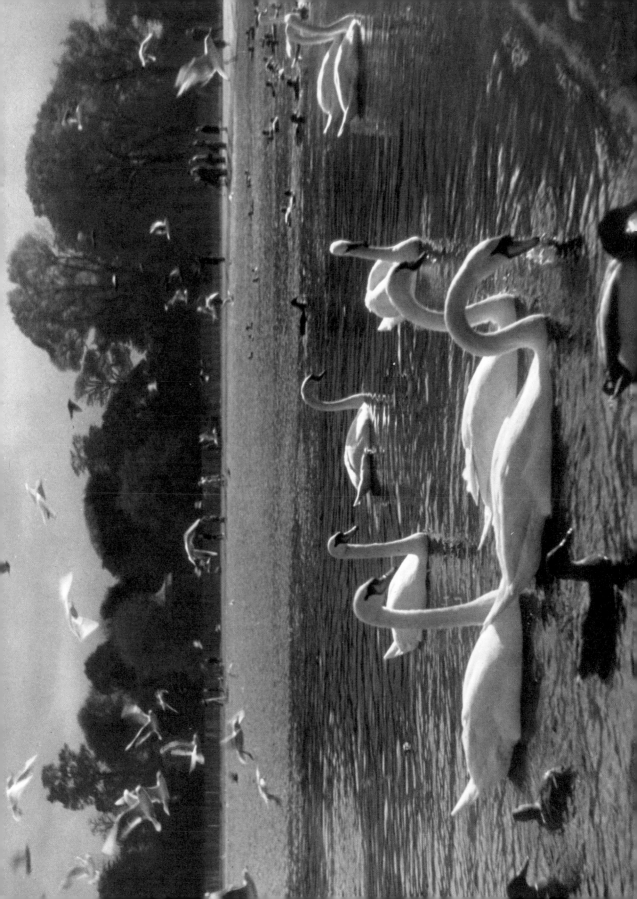

Westminster

The area here photographed is concentrated history—it is also a symphony of "Gothic" in different phases and of different dates: in the distance the Victorian clock tower of the Houses of Parliament, in front of it the diminutive tower of St. Margaret's church, the ground-stage dating from the early sixteenth century though the upper stages, surmounted by an embattled parapet, were rebuilt in the eighteenth century; and then the towers of Westminster Abbey itself, added by John James or Nicholas Hawksmoor (1735–40). The diversity of the architectural scene is further augmented by the Westminster Column in the open space before the Abbey designed by Sir Gilbert Scott and erected (1854–9) to former scholars of Westminster School killed in the Crimean War and Indian Mutiny, St. George and the Dragon surmounting its red granite shaft. Purists have criticised the west front of the Abbey for such details as its "Grecian" pediments and "Tuscan" cornice, yet criticisms of architectural consistency (or its lack) will not prevent the spectator from feeling all the warmth and force of historical association. The outer shell of the Abbey, so much added to during the centuries, conserves the great mediaeval interior, behind the eighteenth-century front extends the superb nave (1350–1420). To the left of the west door is the fourteenth-century Jerusalem Chamber, the Abbot's room when Westminster was, in fact, an Abbey (the room, also, where Henry IV died). St. Margaret's, traditionally the church of the House of Commons, is also—to single out one of its many personal associations, the last resting-place of Sir Walter Raleigh. The Victorian monument stands on or near the site of the house of the first great English printer, William Caxton. Essentially of London is this medley of continued growth and memory, combined as in a living organism.

St. Paul's Cathedral

Since the second Fire of London caused by incendiary bombs in World War II it has been possible to see Sir Christopher Wren's great church (begun in 1675, finished in 1710) from several angles and at close quarters in its completeness. Here is the unobstructed view from the south-east; the dome "huge and dusky", as Hawthorne described it "with here and there a space on its vast form where the original whiteness comes out like a streak of moonshine". Wren achieved its soaring effect by a triple structure, an inner dome, acoustically and otherwise adapted to the interior, above it an intermediate conical dome supporting stone lantern, ball and cross, the outer dome of timber covered with lead being built round the cone. The height from pavement to the gilded cross is 366 feet: the drum on which the dome rests, 139 feet in diameter, adds massiveness to loftiness. The whole length comes into our perspective, the western bell towers in the distance, the choir and south transept in the middle foreground—over the south transept portico is the phoenix carved by Cibber, with the pregnant word "Resurgam" —"I shall rise again" (motto inscribed on a stone from the ruins of the earlier St. Paul's).

Though in 1940 a bomb fell through the roof of the choir, damaging altar and reredos, St. Paul's remains externally as its architect saw it when finished, save, that is, for the weathering of its Portland stone. In the foreground, the low brick wall marks off the bombed area— the inscription "Bread Street" recalls that John Milton was born there in 1608, though his birthplace had disappeared even before *Paradise Lost* was written, destroyed in the Fire of 1666.

BREAD ST

The Houses of Parliament

From the Lambeth embankment one obtains this noble prospect of Westminster, the towers of Westminster Abbey on the one hand and the distant spires of Whitehall Court beyond Westminster Bridge on the other, subordinate to the great central mass of the Houses of Parliament (covering eight acres of ground). Its architect, Sir Charles Barry, by personal inclination favoured formal and classical treatment but in conformity with a prevailing taste for revived Gothic, submitted a winning Gothic design in the competition held after the old building was burned down in 1834. He adhered, however, as can be well appreciated in our photograph to a regular plan, in some contrast with the picturesque diversity of the towers (Perpendicular–Tudor–Victorian) though the whole structure (erected 1840–60) has always commanded admiration and wonder. The Victoria Tower at the south-western corner (420 feet high to the top of the flagstaff), where the flag flies when Parliament is sitting, contains eleven stories in which documents are housed. The towers at the corner nearest the spectator comprise the residences of Black Rod and the Librarian of the House of Lords. The Speaker's residence is at the farther end; between, above the famous Terrace where Members and their guests take tea, are the libraries of the two Houses and a range of committee rooms. The graceful Central Tower containing the ventilating system rises above the Central Hall, separating House of Lords from House of Commons. Big Ben stands at the north-west corner, on the site of Edward I's clock tower. Chemical constituents in the London atmosphere have attacked the dolomitic stone of which the Houses of Parliament are built, crumbling away a good deal of the ornamental detail that lavishly enriched the surface, but long and careful treatment has protected it against further attack, and its warm tone, visually contributes to impressive effects in the soft riverside atmosphere in which artists have always taken delight. Wartime attack, making necessary the reconstruction of the House of Commons, has left no external mark.

Towers of Westminster

The Clock Tower of the Houses of Parliament and the north corner of Westminster Hall are seen in this photograph in impressive relation. Westminster Hall, most important survival from the fire of 1834 which largely destroyed the old Palace of Westminster, was built under William II at the end of the eleventh century, though the old stonework has been several times renewed in the restorations of the eighteenth and nineteenth centuries, and the hand of the Victorian restorer is plainly to be seen in the towers flanking the north entrance at New Palace Yard. The exterior may scarcely prepare the eye for the spectacle of its wonderful timber roof, masterpiece (now happily saved from the death-watch beetle) of Richard II's master carpenter; or the mind for memory of the many historic and moving scenes of which it has been the setting; but the neighbouring Clock Tower of Sir Charles Barry's Houses of Parliament (1840–60), has its immediate visual effect as one of the world's most distinctive architectural symbols.

"Big Ben"—the name is comprehensively applied nowadays to the tower, the clock and the bell that booms out the hours, though strictly it refers to the bell alone, so named after Sir Benjamin Hall, Chief Commissioner of Works when it was hung (1858). Its fourteen tons are suspended from a girder (capable of supporting 100 tons) in the lantern above the clock-face, four smaller bells chiming the quarters. Some statistics are necessary to give scale: the tower is 40 feet square, about 320 feet high; the light in its lantern announcing that Parliament is in session, is 250 feet up and throws its beam for miles; the four clock-faces are 22½ feet in diameter, the figures two feet long, the minute spaces a foot square, the minute hands 14 feet long, the hands travel 100 miles in a year. Yet from a distance the belfry takes on delicacy; the spire tapers finely with a flash of gold.

The Tower

So complete—and even *new*—does the Tower of London look from a distance that in spite of contemporary detail in its surroundings, one seems for a moment to be transported to time long past. The White Tower, central point, keep, fortress, palace, of the concentric system of fortifications comes boldly into view, trees and distance obscuring the surrounding thirteen towers of the Inner Ward and the eight towers of the Outer, though the broad quay with its row of curious antique cannon and its visitors sauntering on its riverside promenade, is well defined. The track of the ancient Roman wall crosses the area from north to south by the White Tower and it may reasonably be assumed that a Roman fort stood here, but the White Tower, the oldest existing part of the structure, is Norman in origin, built by Bishop Gundulf for William the Conqueror, its walls thirteen to fifteen feet thick. It contains the ancient Banqueting Hall, St. John's Chapel, a perfect example of eleventh-century building, and like all the other towers comprised in the single term "the Tower" has its grim and dramatic memories. Here, it is thought the "Princes in the Tower", the sons of Edward IV were murdered; in the Council Chamber Richard II abdicated in favour of Henry IV. Along the river front extends the modern wharf and the series of towers of the Outer Ward—to the left is St. Thomas's Tower and Traitor's Gate, "that gate misnamed through which before, went Sidney, Russell, Raleigh, Cranmer, More". From perforations in the wall, the wardens watched the arrival of state prisoners brought to the then riverside gate by boat. In the photograph we look from Tower Bridge, one of its huge piers is on the right. Dominant in the background on the left is the tower of the Port of London Authority building (opened 1922) designed by Sir Edwin Cooper—office controlling the Thames shipping and its many docks. The Middle Ages, the Victorian age, the twentieth century combine in its historical perspective.

The River and Tower Bridge

The tugs, landing stages, barges, cargo boats and cranes on either side of the Thames frame dramatically the last and easternmost of the Thames bridges, Tower Bridge, that strange and colossal invention of the late nineteenth century. Designed by Sir Horace Jones, the City of London architect (responsible also for Smithfield, the reconstructed Billingsgate and Leadenhall markets, the Guildhall Library and museum) and Sir John Wolfe Barry, civil engineer, it took eight years to build (1886–94), and is equally remarkable as a feat of engineering and a Victorian Gothic fantasy. The towers crowned with pinnacles and spire, that recall the Victoria Tower of Wolfe-Barry's father, Sir Charles Barry at Westminster, are mediaeval-looking, yet their framework is of steel. Permanent spans, 270 feet long, suspended on great chains, connect them with the river bank and smaller castellated towers at the shore approaches. The twin drawbridges or bascules, each weighing 1000 tons, can be raised for the passage of ships by hydraulic machinery in a minute and a half, while 142 feet above the water is an alternative, permanent footway.

As London's watergate it never fails to strike the imagination. On its eastern side, one looks down the opening panorama of dockland. It is flanked, romantically, on one bank by the Tower of London and St. Katherine's Docks, on the other by the warehouses of Pickle Herring Street and Shad Thames. It spans "the Pool", the busy stretch of river that begins below London bridge and extends towards Limehouse Reach. One of the most colourful spectacles that London affords is of the ships moored close alongside it, their holds disgorging bales, casks, commodities of every kind, while the rattle of winches competes with the roar of passing road traffic; and from any angle of its massive piers there is a wonderful view.

East of London Bridge

This is where the Pool begins and the majesty of the Thames is in an enspiriting contrast and combination with the lively and sparkling detail on and alongside either shore—of the cranes, the ocean-going ships that here reach their farthest point west, the lines of barges that swing gently with the tide, the engagingly delicate outline of buildings from which we can still gain some idea of the symphony in stone which Wren intended to compose. Cannon Street Station, beyond London Bridge, thrusts its uncompromising horizontal across the view yet Wren here, as elsewhere, is triumphant—St. Paul's in the distance still asserts itself as the central focus of interest. The eye passes from the dome to the cupola tower and low spire of St. Magnus the Martyr, built between 1676 and 1705, then pauses at the Monument, that fluted column, with its glittering emblem of flame, 202 feet high, and said to be just that distance from the house in Pudding Lane where the Great Fire broke out in 1666, which this noble pillar was built to commemorate (1671–77). To the right is the near-Gothic, lantern-like steeple of St. Dunstan's in the East (1699). These delicacies of late seventeenth-century architecture rise with their individual precision from the dense mass of lanes and warehouses, serene above the tumult and swishing hoses of Billingsgate Market, the decorous façade and broad quay of the Custom House. Shipping, architecture, historical association make, at this point of the river, for a singular concentration of interest.

Cheyne Walk

In Cheyne Walk, that famous stretch of houses overlooking the Chelsea Embankment and the river, one can best study the eighteenth-century architecture of the region, while here also are concentrated many of its vivid associations with painters, writers and others who have given Chelsea its special lustre. At No. 118–19, charmingly cottage-like in effect, Turner lodged in his old age and observed the atmospheric effects of the river from the roof. John Martin, painter of awesome, apocalyptic pictures, studied romantic moonlight from the balcony of Lindley House, late seventeenth-century mansion, divided into separate dwellings. Whistler lived in its east wing, No. 96, and elsewhere on Cheyne Walk. The Pre-Raphaelite household of Dante Gabriel Rossetti, at No. 16, gives a stirring chapter to Chelsea's story. Wilson Steer, leader among British Impressionists, lived for forty-four years at No. 109. Cheyne Walk was the favourite promenade of Thomas Carlyle, who lived for so long in Cheyne Row, and described with affection the "Parade", running along the shore of the river, "a broad highway with huge shady trees, boats lying moored and a smell of shipping and tar"; at a later date it was no less attractive to Henry James who lived at 21 Carlyle Mansions. The Embankment now separates Cheyne Walk from the river with some loss of picturesqueness but the huge shady trees remain, and a number of the early Georgian houses, dating from about 1705–17—a good example is seen behind the plane tree in our photograph—often with fine eighteenth-century gates and railings. There is still, in the delightful brickwork and design of such houses, interrupted as the river frontage is to some extent by more recent flats (and the gaps caused by bombing), something of the character of an old Dutch town.

Piccadilly Circus

Piccadilly Circus at the present day is a scene unrivalled in London for colour and movement. The hearty red of the buses that seem to shoulder their way through the surging traffic round its island, the bright buff walls of the Pavilion corner, the multi-hued electric signs (that have a colour scheme of their own by day as well as night) combine in gaiety of effect: while "Eros", the Shaftesbury Memorial Fountain, adds its own period gaiety, the flavour of the nineties. Analysed, from an architectural point of view the Circus is a strange miscellany, and as a piece of town planning notably imperfect. The imposing buildings at the end of the proudly curving Regent Street Quadrant, Swan and Edgar's and its arcaded *vis-à-vis* have nothing in common with the nondescript buildings of the 1880s on the Glasshouse Street and Shaftesbury Avenue side—the obscure backgrounds in our photograph of Guinness, Bovril and Coca-cola. The congested road space may be unfavourably compared with the admirable circus beneath it—of London's Underground. On the other hand it remains indisputably the western centre; as a great crossroads; because of all the associations that have grown round it, and of the clusters of theatres and restaurants that bring to it an unending succession of pleasure-seekers. The fountain and statue designed by Sir Alfred Gilbert and unveiled in 1893 form a distinguished central point, unique among London's sculptures in the respect accorded it as a work of art and its place in the affections of the public. It is one of the Circus's two memorials to the philanthropic Earl of Shaftesbury, the broad Shaftesbury Avenue stemming from it, and dating from 1886, being the other. Sir Alfred's masterpiece was an ungrateful and expensive task for him, but he lived until 1934, to see it the best beloved of London's monuments.

Trafalgar Square

Silhouetted in the foreground, one of Sir Edwin Landseer's famous lions at the foot of the Nelson Column looks (as it has done since 1868) amiably towards one of the fountains (added to the square in 1948 and designed by Sir Edwin Lutyens) that sends up a cool mist of spray over the strollers watching the antics of the pigeons. And towards the bronze equestrian statue of George IV by Sir Francis Chantrey, originally intended for the top of the Marble Arch, and installed here in 1845; beyond it towards the Coliseum in St. Martin's Lane (the great ball, above it, a landmark of theatreland). Begun in 1830, Trafalgar Square effected a clearance of a tangle of slums and has remained more of an open place than any other London square: arriving at its present appearance by a leisurely process of accretion and improvement. The National Gallery, was built on the site of the old King's Mews (1832–8) and though it incorporated the dignified columns from Carlton House, the various features which exposed the design by William Wilkins to much criticism are of curious interest in our photograph, notably one of its "pepper-boxes without pepper", which caused it formerly to be described as "the National Cruet". The Nelson Column was erected no earlier than the 1840s, the statues of nineteenth-century heroes, Napier, by Adams, Havelock, by Behnes, Gordon, by Hamo Thornycroft, at later intervals. It was planted with trees in 1879, a line of them being then continued along Northumberland Avenue to the Embankment. The trees now pleasantly soften the severity of its granite terraces, it has as a whole a cool magnificence and a varied series of prospects, from this colourful view looking to the north, to the prospect of Whitehall from the National Gallery's portico.

St. Martin-in-the-Fields

In singular beauty St. Martin-in-the-Fields, masterpiece of the architect, James Gibbs, presides to the east of Trafalgar Square, accommodating itself with graceful ease to propinquity with many sorts of architecture, the squat dome and uncertain cupolas and turrets of the National Gallery, the grandiose frivolity of the Coliseum, the bulk of South Africa House. It stands on the site of a church built in the reign of Henry VIII and then, literally, "in the fields", though the district was both populous and distinguished when the old church was pulled down in 1721 and the present building erected—"a decent tabernacle", said the *London Spy* in 1725, "which can produce as handsome a show of white hands, diamond rings, pretty snuff-boxes and gilt prayer books as any cathedral whatever". St. Martin's was the royal parish, the birth of princes and princesses entered in the church's register and hence the royal coat of arms in the pediment over the most handsome of London's Corinthian porticoes. Critics have observed that the steeple seems to rest on no apparent foundation, but if this is an aesthetic error, few people would be aware of it in looking at the delightful steeple itself. When Trafalgar Square was laid out, St. Martin's stood in the midst of a crowded slum area picturesquely named "the Bermudas"; still hemmed in on three sides it has the advantage of an open space before it and "civic improvements" have not ventured to attack the steps leading up to the porch. Neighbouring St. Martin's Lane was the artist's quarter of old London and many artists were buried at St. Martin's—Hogarth and Reynolds, for example, attended the funeral of Roubiliac in 1762. Associations are many. Sir Winston Churchill, father of the great Duke of Marlborough, was buried in 1688 in the narrow churchyard that is now a children's playground. The crypt, a refuge of the homeless in the days of pre-war Depression, was a shelter and place of refreshment during the war years. St. Martin's has long been admired as a centre of warm humanity as well as a work of art.

Grosvenor Square

The fashionable squares of Mayfair have greatly changed in the twentieth century, and though Grosvenor Square has not been so drastically altered as the east side of Berkeley Square by towering offices it has taken on a modern character—or at least modern buildings dominate, even if old houses remain to recall the pomp of Georgian and Victorian days. It dates back to the early eighteenth century, when it was the most westerly of the city's aristocratic additions, and long resisted change—not until 1842 did it admit gas lamps instead of oil, being the last London square to do so—its link-extinguishers have long been celebrated as a memory of the time when "link boys" were the necessary attendants of a fashionable evening party. Equally, a wrought-iron balcony may recall its height of Victorian splendour. Latterly it has been a symbol of Anglo-American friendship. The American Embassy is on its eastern side, automobiles of trans-atlantic design and colour enliven its roadways, successors to the American army vehicles that filled it in wartime. The ambassador in World War I, Walter Page, here penned his championship of Britain: and grateful respect for the memory of Franklin Roosevelt has, since World War II, placed in the gardens of the square the statue of the President by Sir William Reid Dick. It is the twentieth-century aspect of the square that is seen in our photograph and the plane trees and lawns in the spacious gardens (originally laid out by William Kent) make a dignified setting for the statue of the great man.

Belgrave Square

Belgrave Square retains that look of opulence which associates it with the high noon of the Victorian age and is indeed the archetype of Victorian expansion, with its columned porches and its variations on the classical theme, its occasional balconies and first-floor pavilions; though it is pre-Victorian in date. The purchase of Buckingham House by George III foretold a westward move of fashion, though the King himself was dissuaded from buying the fields behind the palace, with the result that Grosvenor Place (built 1767) overlooks the palace grounds. The marshy land, beyond, known as the Five Fields, haunt of eighteenth-century highwaymen, seemed a poor bargain for Earl Grosvenor but in 1825 soil brought from the excavations of St. Katherine's Docks gave a firmer substance to the marsh and Belgrave Square was built to the design of the architect George Basevi, pupil of the classical Sir John Soane. It was named, like other new streets and squares in the region, after a title and property of the Grosvenor family, "Belgravia", like Mayfair, acquiring its own social implications. Nearness to Buckingham Palace and its princely scale and plan including the detached mansions at the angles (one of which is seen in our photograph) made it the abode of titled persons, foreigners of distinction, and embassies. In the twentieth century it has maintained its tradition, though to one side of it a curving block of modern flats proclaims an altered conception of design and domestic living. Not the most beautiful of London squares, architecturally it has an air of dignity, and if the cars in our photograph be mentally replaced by broughams and landaus one might imagine it still as basking in Victorian sunshine.

Montagu Square

This charming square, part of the development of the Portman estate north of Oxford Street, is one of the pleasant discoveries to be made in domestic London, though in the days of Victorian splendour it was regarded with some contempt for its modest aspect. It is a companion to Bryanston Square and both date back to 1811. Late in the nineteenth century they were described in the *Builder* as "mere oblong slips with houses built in dreary uniformity; they are fortunately out of the way and few people see them". They are in fact in the grand tradition of the Adam brothers, that extends, a visible influence in this region from Portman Square, lingering in Baker Street and still evident in the neighbouring Gloucester Place. The uniformity to the modern eye is an agreeably ordered simplicity, and tempered in Montagu Square by the shallow bow windows.

Bryanston Square, like other squares on the Portman property (Dorset, Orchard, Blandford) was named after one of the family's country houses. Montagu Square has a more personal derivation—after the celebrated Mrs. Montagu, "Queen of the Bluestockings" and friend of Dr. Johnson, for whom the classically-minded architect, James ("Athenian") Stuart designed (*c*. 1780) Montagu House at the north-west angle of Portman Square. Montagu House was destroyed in World War II (when Montagu Square was extensively occupied by the American Forces). The square now looks as placid and assured in its modest elegance, as if no stirring events had disturbed its serenity since the early nineteenth century.

Old Bond Street

Bond Street is an atmosphere; an atmosphere of luxury and art, hardly to be described in architectural terms. It is narrow. It has no observable plan or design, no dominant feature catches the eye. Though it was built originally at the end of the seventeenth century by Sir Thomas Bond, Comptroller of the Household to Henrietta Maria, no trace of this historic past is to be found in its façades; and though it has had distinguished residents— Laurence Sterne died in Bond Street and Nelson lived there for a time—it is now to be thought of mainly in terms of shopping. Its shops are both dignified and unobtrusive, many of them none the less endearing to the modern eye for their Edwardian chic; the very faintly, old-world front of Atkinson's and the smartly rectangular *Time* and *Life* building (with its reliefs by Henry Moore) are twentieth-century additions that Bond Street quietly assimilates, though the new Westbury Hotel is a modern challenge to old-fashioned character. To explain Bond Street's aroma of quality with any precision one must consider its windows, so calmly conscious, in the reticence of display, of superiority. At frequent intervals one comes to the galleries of art dealers, internationally famous; that Italian "primitive", that eighteenth-century English portrait; that French Impressionist, decorously and singly shown, noble samples of masterpieces within, would add up in vulgar monetary terms to many thousands of pounds. With a different, but still a real reverence, one may contemplate the masterly confection of a tie, the exquisite finish of hand-made shoes. There are all sorts of things in Bond Street (though it may be less the head-quarters of fashion design than Grosvenor Street and Bruton Street), perfumes, jewellery, tobacco, tweeds, but mostly of the best. It is hard to imagine from its present aspect its appearance as a fashionable promenade in the eighteenth century. A fashionable promenade of limited pavement, choked with buses and cars, is something of a contradiction, but the aristocratic air clings to it even in this crowding and democratic age.

Shepherd Market

Coming from the narrow lane out of Piccadilly, called White Horse Street we arrive at this little "village in Mayfair", Shepherd's Market, cosily enclosed. An archway at the farther end provides an entrance and at the same time cuts it off from the more metropolitan dignity of Curzon Street. It is only a market in the sense that it has its own cluster of small shops. The original market was a feature of the May Fair, held in the eighteenth century on May Day and giving the district its name. The fair, however, was not attended by shepherds: a Mr. Shepherd owned the ground on which the May Fair was held and Shepherd's Market built. As a "village" it is wonderfully complete; one need not walk more than a few yards to visit grocer, butcher, fishmonger, fruiterer, newsagent, chemist, though in its delightful inner court and round its edges, there are antique shops full of the cottage ornaments and other charming trifles of the past which perhaps will tempt the owner of some newly-confected "bijou" residence in a Mayfair mews. There are, in plenty, those cafés of a homely, cockney kind, catering inexpensively for what has become a commercial as well as a fashionable area—but something of the chic of fashionable Mayfair has infiltrated, the plain, somewhat stolid architecture contrasts with an occasional smartness of décor and the "continental" frivolity represented by a striped awning and open-air café tables. Full of incident and colour, Shepherd Market has the most local of characters.

Clubland

Dr. Johnson's definition of a club as "an assembly of good fellows, under certain conditions", covers, but not very explicitly, the desire for society—or seclusion—the sharing of kindred interests, political or otherwise which, mainly in the nineteenth century, created a whole chain of palaces in the West End of London, with associations conservative, liberal, military and naval, literary and academic. It is the United Services Club we see at the eastern corner of Waterloo Place in this photograph, designed by John Nash (who was also responsible for laying out Waterloo Place itself) with the touch of the grandiose he knew so well how to give, though some later improvements were added by Decimus Burton. The United Services Club was formed after Waterloo in 1815, when many officers of the army and navy were thrown out of commission and required a meeting-place where they could enjoy familiar amenities and company: the success of the scheme, reflected in the number of candidates and growth of funds, allowed the erection of these palatial premises in 1828. The Athenæum at the opposite corner of Waterloo Place (its shadow falls at the right of our picture) followed in 1830. Designed by Decimus Burton, its statue of Pallas Athene and its adaptation of the Parthenon frieze provide a classical complement to the frieze and the figure of Britannia in the pediment of the United Services. The famous clubhouses stretch westward along Pall Mall in chronological succession but in the photograph we stand at the eastern end of "clubland" where it merges into the region of travel agencies and shipping lines in Cockspur Street—and at the end of the vista, the dome of the National Gallery looks its mild and inoffensive best.

Hyde Park Gardens

It might be said that John Nash (1752–1835) changed the colour of London by his addiction to that plaster coating for wall surfaces known as stucco—material so extensively used by all and sundry in the early nineteenth century and one of the decisive distinctions of aspect between the domestic regions that grew up round Hyde Park and the old eighteenth-century London of brick. The words "Regency" and "stucco" go together, though "Regency" was a style of transition somewhat elastic in its boundaries. In the narrow terms of the Regency Act, it would apply to the period between 1810 and 1820, but style did not abruptly alter when the Prince Regent became George IV nor when he died in 1830; and in fact had gathered an impetus that took it on into Victorian times. In town architecture as well as details of furniture and decoration the transition from Regency to Victorian was gentle. It may be studied in the region once called "Tyburnia", between Edgware Road and Westbourne Terrace, which came into existence in the reign of William IV. In the Regency proper, the northern boundary of the metropolis finished where the Marble Arch stands. It was by later degrees, that, as the Rev. J. Richardson observed in 1856 "tea gardens and other similar low haunts of debauchery", gave way to the elegant and stately buildings with which it (region west and north-west of Marble Arch) is now covered. Of these, Hyde Park Gardens, at the back of Hyde Park Place, is a good example. Middle-class mansions for large families and numerous servants, they kept moderate vestiges of aristocratic architecture, and of the luxury of trees that went with it. The pedimented windows and pillars speak of "Tyburnia's" respectful rivalry with Belgravia.

Park Lane

The air of private and Victorian luxury still clings to remaining old houses in Park Lane, with their white bow fronts and wrought-iron verandas and balconies, though as a whole this one-sided street, privileged in its view over the expanse of Hyde Park, has in recent times undergone such great changes, and been transformed largely into offices, hotels and flats. The huge Dorchester Hotel replaces the old Dorchester House, a mansion of the 1850s, famous for Mr. Holford's splendid collection of old masters. Grosvenor House replaces the Georgian mansion of the same name, once the town residence of the Duke of Westminster and also noted for its gallery of superb paintings, the collection begun by Richard, first Earl Grosvenor. There are remaining mansions that speak of millionaire occupancy as late as the 1930s, but Park Lane as a whole, fashionable still, is as far as its old houses are concerned an emblem of a vanished or vanishing order. An interest, not only of architecture or wealth, attaches to the corner house of Park Lane and Upper Grosvenor Street the residence of Disraeli for more than thirty years, including the period of his first Premiership. It had previously belonged to his Parliamentary colleague, Wyndham Lewis, whose widow he married in 1839. He left it after her death. It is now occupied by offices. Many have been the changes since Park Lane was "the lane leading from Piccadilly to Tyburn" in the reign of Queen Anne, a lonely and straggling rural stretch. The old houses reach the end of their span of social life but the excellence of its position gives Park Lane the promise of splendour continued, if of a new kind.

Hyde Park Corner and Apsley House

At Hyde Park Corner in the early morning, before the immense tide of traffic has begun to circle round its islands (the horseman in our picture is evidently bound for a ride in Rotten Row), one can appreciate the dignified architectural group formed by the screen entrance to the Park and Apsley House next to it; and reflect on the many links here to be found with the great Duke of Wellington. The Achilles statue by Westmacott just within the Park was erected in 1822 in his honour. The equestrian statue of the Duke by Boehm (just outside our line of vision) faces the house. The triumphal arch, moved in 1883 to Constitution Hill, was formerly surmounted by the subject of a famous controversy, another huge equestrian statue of the Duke, now banished to Aldershot and replaced by Adrian Jones's Quadriga, symbolising Peace. The house itself remains the principal Wellingtonian monument. An Adam building (1777–8) it was bought by the Duke from his brother in 1817. At much personal expense he faced it with Bath stone, added the Corinthian portico and made various extensions. Frivolously known as "No. 1, London", Apsley House (otherwise, 149 Piccadilly) was presented to the nation by the present Duke in 1947, and after World War II damage had been repaired, and considerable renovation, was opened as the Wellington Museum in 1952. The Waterloo Gallery, part of the west wing added in 1828–9, where the Waterloo (reunion) Banquets were held from 1830 to 1852; containing many of the old master paintings looted from the Spanish Royal Collections and retrieved by the Duke at the Battle of Vittoria from Joseph Bonaparte's baggage train; is one of its main attractions. The Triple Gateway to the west that consorts in appearance so well with Apsley House, was designed by Decimus Burton and built at the same time as the Duke's additions to the house (1828). The classical interests of that period are marked by the adaptation of the Parthenon frieze carved over the central entrance way.

St. James's Park

St. James's Park has changed much in appearance since the days of Charles II. It was then laid out in the style of Le Nôtre with formally spaced avenues of elms and limes and a long, straight canal. Its present aspect is due to John Nash (1827–9) who gave it its winding water and "composed" it like a natural landscape, with such delightfully rural effect as is seen in our photograph. Yet one is bound to think a little of its early history. The "red deere", "Guinea goates" and "Arabian sheepe" that Evelyn remarked on in 1664, have gone but the "severall sorts of ordinary and extraordinary wild fowle" remain, including the pelican and some direct descendants of the birds introduced by Charles II. "Duck Island" at the east reminds us of the sinecure (no doubt laughingly) bestowed by Charles on St. Evremond—Governor of Duck Island. Charles walked in the park unattended and it has since been the quiet exercise-ground of illustrious men—many a Prime Minister has taken his solitary morning walk, turning over the problems of Downing Street, on the shores of the lake. If one thinks of the past, even the seats where visitors take their ease may recall those equally popular in Oliver Goldsmith's time where "if a man be splenetic he may every day meet companions, with whose groans he may mix his own and pathetically talk of the weather".

In either direction there is a superb view from the miniature suspension bridge that crosses the water—towards Buckingham Palace at one end of the park and towards the Foreign Office and the domes and turrets strangely assembled at the other. The weeping willows by the shore have an Oriental delicacy; in all seasons Nature is the more poignant in effect for being thus islanded here in the heart of London.

St. James's Park and Horse Guards Parade

The small scale of St. James's Park does not take away from but rather increases the variety of interest it affords. One can appreciate like the detail of a miniature, the gay flower-beds, the exotic waterfowl, the little lake and the trees so artfully disposed by John Nash (in the reign of George IV) that they seem to become a spacious natural landscape. Alternatively, it is a vantage point from which to obtain unique glimpses of London's buildings, of Buckingham Palace and the Victoria Memorial casting their reflections in the waters of the lake, or the distant gleam of Whitehall, Whitehall Court and the National Liberal Club, a cluster of spires like those of some palace of dreams. In our photograph we are at the eastern end of the park. The foreground patch of green a little recalls the grassy walks of an earlier day along which Charles II liked to saunter. Behind the bank of flowers to the left is the Guards Memorial of the First World War by Gilbert Ledward, a cenotaph, on the farther side of which stand five guardsmen (in bronze melted down from captured German guns). Beyond, the open space of the Horse Guards Parade provides an intimate, an "inside" view of official Whitehall. The low façade and clock tower of William Kent's Horse Guards, built in 1742, directly ahead, are brilliant in Portland stone. And here also is one of London's most picturesque skylines. The tops of the nineteenth-century buildings behind Whitehall add their fantasy to classic design and give the illusion of being part of a complex fairy-tale fabric.

The Strand Churches

The two beautiful churches on islands in the Strand, St. Clement Danes and St. Mary-le-Strand, were both damaged in World War II. The outer shell of St. Clement Danes keeps a seeming perfection until one peers through the windows at a bare, roofless interior. In our photograph, St. Clement Danes, the elder of the two, built in 1689 under the supervision of Sir Christopher Wren, with a spire in diminishing stages added later by Gibbs, is seen against the background of the Law Courts. Nearer to the spectator and flanked by the southern aspect of Bush House is St. Mary-le-Strand (1714–27) entirely the work of Gibbs and first of the churches authorised to be built in the reign of Queen Anne. In this, St. Martin-in-the-Fields, and St. Clement Danes, Gibbs shows himself a master of the steeple in slender and graceful variations. It was in St. Clement's that Dr. Johnson attended service, "repeating the responses in the Litany with tremulous energy". A statue of the great man survives in the tiny churchyard. Association of an earlier church with the early Danish settlements has been suggested to explain the poetic but mysterious name. An old St. Mary-le-Strand seems to have occupied the site of the eastern part of Somerset House: the present church to have been built where the old Maypole stood, 100 feet high. The Puritans, enemies not only of dancing and festivity but of its pagan symbolism did away with it in 1664, though a still taller Maypole was erected at this spot at the Restoration "at which the little children did much rejoice, and ancient people did clap their hands, saying golden days began to appear". The Maypole was finally removed when the church was built, the exchange being ironically the subject of comment in Pope's *Dunciad*. St. Mary-le-Strand no longer collects "the saints of Drury Lane" but its beauty is a relief to the eye in the busy modern thoroughfare.

The Law Courts

The Royal Courts of Justice (by formal description), last of the great, secular nineteenth-century buildings to be designed in the "Gothic" style, presents a fretted surface of white Portland stone to the Strand, giving an impression of weight and majesty undiminished by the number of pinnacles, turrets and pointed arches that break the façade of some 500 feet in length. The major work of George Edmund Street, who was appointed its architect in 1868, it was opened in 1882, though the architect did not live to see its completion. Street's ideal in architecture was fourteenth-century English Gothic, but the somewhat irregular aspect of the Law Courts was not intended merely to appear ancient; he believed, like other Victorian devotees of Gothic that the style expressed "function" better than the symmetrical, "classic" building which did not externally distinguish one part, or purpose, from another. The functional problem involved in these five acres of stone and brick, extending in a rough square from Carey Street to the Strand, was a large one. He had to plan, as well as the imposing Central Hall (138 feet long by 48 feet wide), nineteen distinct courtrooms (the number has since been added to), each with its own entrance and staircase, separate ways of access for judge, jury, witnesses, the Bar and public, together with rooms for clerks, secretaries and registrars and also waiting rooms. More than 1100 apartments of one sort or another are represented by its varied window spaces. These functional matters give point to the comment of *The Times* in 1874 (when the first stone, after many delays, was laid) that the "architect has embodied in his designs so much of modern improvements and has so thoroughly studied the adaptation of the Edwardian period (Edward II, Edward III) to the requirements of our age that we fancy he would prefer to call the structure a specimen of the 'Victorian style'". A new wing was added in 1913 at the west end, where space was prudently allowed for possible extensions; but of this remarkable structure as a whole, fascinating to study as a phase of the Victorian outlook, it is probably true to say we shall not look upon its like again.

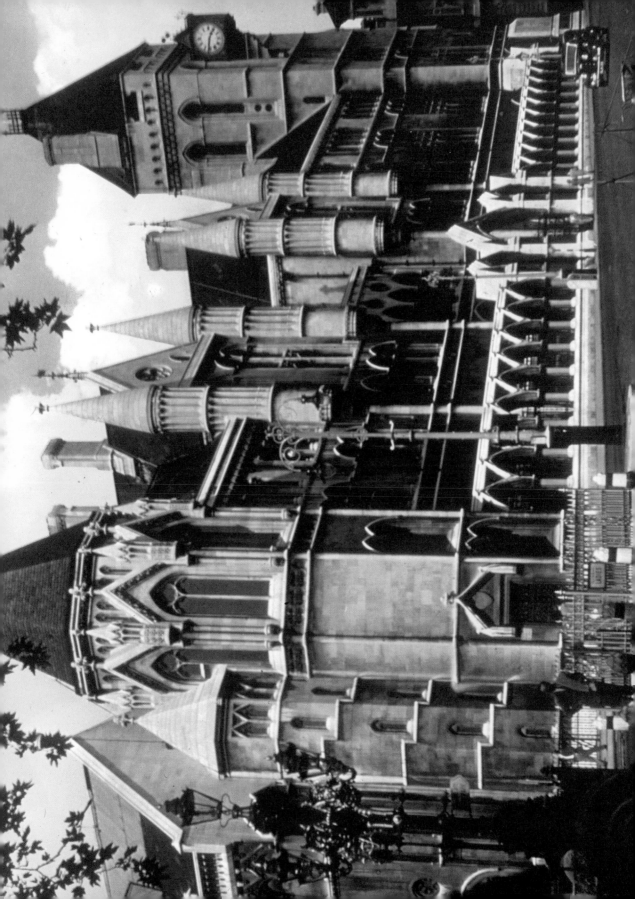

Fleet Street

From its slight mound, little Ludgate Hill, St. Paul's benignly commands the vista of Fleet Street, its double portico of twin Corinthian columns inset between buildings on either side. In front of its western towers is the thin, graceful steeple of St. Martin's, built by Wren in 1684, with square tower and timber spire, still giving point to an old verse:

> *"Lo, like a bishop upon dainties fed*
> *St. Paul lifts up his sacerdotal head;*
> *While his lean curates, slim and lank to view*
> *Around him point their steeples to the blue."*

At the foot of Ludgate Hill, where a bridge anciently crossed the Fleet River (now a sewer running underground) is the Railway viaduct that by long familiarity seems hardly to spoil the handsome prospect beyond it. And then the "Street of Ink" itself, the whole world of journalism concentrated in the narrow thoroughfare and in the narrower streets and courts round it. On the right is Reuters, nerve centre of News, with its impressively arched entrance. A little turning here brings us to St. Bride's, rebuilt by Wren after the Fire and left a shell by modern war—the church in which (appropriately in view of Fleet Street's later associations) Caxton's pupil, the printer-publisher, Wynkyn de Worde was buried. The Street is miscellaneous in its architecture, from the remarkable black-glazed modern front of a famous newspaper at the corner of Shoe Lane, to the early nineteenth-century belfry of St. Dunstan's. It is equally noted for its many taverns, "Cock", "Mitre", "Rainbow", "Cheshire Cheese", with the savour of history in their names; as for the numerous teashops, dairies and milkbars that refresh the modern journalist. The quaint courts and alleys with which it is seamed are full of literary associations—one cannot, when Fleet Street is at its busiest, quite forget Boswell in Wine Office Court, or Dr. Johnson in Gough Square, but the press photographs, of planes, football matches and beauty queens in the newspaper offices are its dominant images.

Guildhall

As a meeting-place of the guilds, for the transaction of City business and the election of its officers, a court, and a banqueting hall where the City entertains distinguished people, the Guildhall has a history going back at least to the thirteenth century, though it has been several times reconstructed. The oldest remaining parts are the crypt and the interior porch of the building erected in the fifteenth century and the reign of Henry IV. Externally, however, what we see is an early essay in the revival of Gothic (1789) by George Dance the younger (1741–1825), quaint rather than splendid architecturally and fiercely criticised by the learned devotees of Gothic in the Victorian age. The main magnificence of the Guildhall has always resided in the great interior chamber, 150 feet long. Its roof was destroyed in the Great Fire of 1666 (there is a vivid description of the timbers glowing but still in position "like a palace of gold"), in Dance's time there was a makeshift; the roof was restored in 1864 by Sir Horace Jones, with a central louvre and tapering metal spire. Incendiary bombs ruined this restoration in December 1940 (when the carved figures of the legendary City giants, Gog and Magog were buried under the rubble). The spire is new, the interior was again completely restored by Sir Giles Gilbert Scott in 1954. The Library (Gothic of 1871) with its great collection of prints and books relating to London survives, the Museum brings Roman discoveries in the City up to date, the Art Gallery is still of note for its paintings of scenes of pageantry and ceremony in London.

At the corner of the Guildhall yard is the church of St. Laurence Jewry, rebuilt (1671–80) in sumptuous fashion by Sir Christopher Wren who was also responsible for the Guildhall Alderman's Court Room (decorated by Sir James Thornhill).

Heart of the City

The new Bank of England, designed by Sir Herbert Baker, rises on the left above the windowless façade of the old. The learned Sir John Soane, architect to the Bank from 1788 to 1827, adapted his one-story front from the Temple of Vesta at Tivoli, and made it windowless for security reasons, lighting it from inner courts. A freer and more opulent classicism marks the twentieth-century addition that surges up in a great block, broken by varied colonnades from the four acres the Bank covers. Six figures by the modern sculptor, Charles Wheeler with such allegorical suggestion as key and cornucopia can convey are ranged above the doorway while on the pediment, the "Lady of Threadneedle Street", up to date, sits with a model of the Bank on her knee amid the wealth of the world. Neighbouring is the Royal Exchange, on its triangular site between Threadneedle Street, Cornhill and Poultry. It looks older than its actual age, having been built no longer ago than 1842–4 by Sir William Tite, and is the third Exchange to stand on the site, for the convenience, to use the words of the London chronicler, Stow, of "the merchants and tradesmen as well English as strangers . . . for their general making of bargains, contracts and commerce". In one way and another its practical function has been usurped by other institutions, it remains an impressive memory of the past. The grasshopper on the windvane above its bell-tower—the Gresham crest—recalls the founder of the first Exchange, Sir Thomas Gresham, whose statue is on the eastern side of the campanile. The scene offers sculpture in plenty; in front of the Exchange we see Chantrey's equestrian statue of the Duke of Wellington, on the pediment above, Commerce (by Sir Richard Westmacott) welcoming the nations. The inscription below the central figure, "The Earth is the Lord's and the fulness thereof" was chosen by Dean Milman, on the suggestion of the Prince Consort that some mark of respect be shown to a Superior Power.

"Petticoat Lane"

The destruction of a good many buildings, and the appearance (about 1935) of modernistic streamlined emporia, have taken from Middlesex Street something of its old sooty and narrow canyon-like atmosphere, but the serried stalls, the closely packed crowds, when the famous Sunday market is in swing, affirm its traditional character. The name of the street has been changed twice; it was Hog Lane when the chronicler, Stow described it, in the seventeenth century, as a row of semi-rural cottages. It was Petticoat Lane in the nineteenth century when its name had become descriptive. It was then as Mayhew observed in his *London Labour and the London Poor* "essentially the old clothes district . . . a vista of many-coloured dinginess as regards female attire . . . while incessantly threading their way through all this intricacy is a mass of people, some of whose dresses speak of a recent purchase in this lane". As Middlesex Street (a "ludicrous" alias in the view of Augustus Hare in his *Walks in London*) it is no longer devoted to old clothes, though the new dresses to be seen behind those long horizontal panes of glass are a reminder that Whitechapel is a centre of the clothing industry. There are dresses to be bought still in the market itself but it has long ceased to be specialised, has become a fair and an entertainment for visitors to London and Londoners from all quarters. It is one of the most dramatic sensations that the capital provides to come through the deserted city on a Sunday to this bustling scene of the East End, bustling, that is, in vividness and noise, though movement, in the dense throng with its motionless knots of people listening to the raucous patter of salesmen, is strictly limited. All sorts of commodities—useful and useless—and its variety of sightseers, give it abounding and exciting colour.

Buckingham Palace and Sentry

Buckingham Palace is closed to sightseers: but at its gates the visitor finds epitomised the dignity of state. Ceremony, discipline, order, tradition, military and civil, they are severally represented by the "man in blue" and the guardsman in red and blue, wearing his bearskin, who swings by the gate with movements of controlled precision, a fashion-plate of military full dress. The forecourt is the traditional morning scene of the Changing of the Guard, splendid in colour and rhythm, when the New Guard advances to the sound of drum and fife, the sentries are relieved and posted and the band strikes up with stirring vigour as the Old Guard marches back to barracks.

The open side gate (the central gates are never opened) is fittingly ceremonial in itself, with its golden fleurs-de-lis, its lion-crowned coat of arms with pendant medallion of St. George and the Dragon, its flanking stone piers, elaborately carved with dolphins, cherubs and varied emblems; though the façade of the Palace, glimpsed behind is simpler in character. It has been several times reconstructed since George III bought the old Buckingham House in 1762. John Nash began the rebuilding in 1825 for George IV, but with a pompous and somewhat fantastic effect, increased by the Marble Arch (then forming part of its composition) and much disliked by William IV. The east front was redesigned by Blore in 1846, the Marble Arch being removed to its present site after its completion. The stucco front was once again replaced in 1913 by the stone front redesigned by Sir Aston Webb. Its present aspect is thus comparatively new, and a gain in dignity.

Sentry at the Horse Guards

The mounted sentries in their stone recesses at the Horse Guards, Whitehall, are an everyday, a famous, and always a fascinating spectacle. A book of London in colour would not be entirely complete without the colour of that uniform in its startlingly unmodern brilliance, the scarlet tunic, the white gauntlets and buckskin breeches, the sweeping plume, the gleaming helmet and cuirass, the glossy riding-boots that in their archaic design take us back to the seventeenth century. We must look to the seventeenth century for the origin of this phenomenon among the government offices of Whitehall, for it was then that Charles II formed a troop of "Horse Guards" for the protection of the King's person. They were accommodated in stables and barracks in the old Tilt Yard, or parade and exercise ground between Whitehall and St. James's Park. These buildings were pulled down to make way for the permanent quarters erected in 1742 and designed by William Kent—later than the adjoining old Admiralty but earlier than the street-screen in front of the latter by Robert Adam (which in appearance harmonises with the Horse Guards so well). Tradition has preserved both the uniform and the ancient duty though the building is now simply an extra suite of government offices, and the sentries do not challenge the movement of pedestrians through the gates and archway to and from Whitehall and Horse Guards Parade. Pageantry becomes active when the Guard is changed at eleven in the morning and the New Guard walk their horses across the Parade. The sentries and their horses, motionless in position, represent a triumph of discipline.

Queen Anne's Gate

Between St. James's Park and Tothill Street, Westminster, it is a delight to come, in the quiet backwater of Queen Anne's Gate, on houses such as these—which may be called "Augustan" in belonging to and so well representing the Augustan age of Queen Anne. The harmony of design linking them is a notable feature—the street was laid out as a whole, about 1704, and originally known as Queen's Square. Though some alterations have since been made they are not extensive enough to affect the general harmony and dignity of proportion of the houses on its north and south sides and at its west end: and the small statue of Queen Anne on a pedestal at one corner endorses the period character. The tall windows are very distinguished, the grotesque masks on the keystones above the ground- and first-floor windows, worthy of individual note. The carved Doric pilasters and original, richly carved hoods to some of the doorways give an effect of unusual magnificence—they might be called "museum pieces" (one doorway is now in the Victoria and Albert Museum). The brickwork has mellowed beautifully. It is a commentary on the strange fluctuations of taste, that nineteenth century remarks on these buildings so often denied them beauty and conceded, at most, that they were in appearance "comfortable" and "solid". To the modern eye it is rather stateliness, refinement of form and luxury of detail that are their special characteristics. Queen Anne's Gate has no particular association with famous people of the eighteenth century but it comes near, as far as a few houses can do, to conveying to us the essence of an historical period.

Kensington Palace

The least palatial of royal palaces, in its domestic scale, its plain red brick, Kensington Palace quietly asserts the virtues of simplicity. It developed out of the "Nottingham House", bought and rebuilt in 1661 by Heneage Finch who became Earl of Nottingham. William III bought Nottingham House in 1689 (considering the air of Kensington good for his asthma) and commissioned Sir Christopher Wren to reconstruct and add to it. Further additions and alterations were made in the eighteenth century, the whole building, roughly rectangular, enclosing a series of courts: "Clock Court", behind the south-west front (with its clock tower of 1691), retaining some part of the original structure. Wren in his most restrained mood established the unobtrusive character of the exterior, though the staterooms within called for, and recived, more sumptuous treatment. Mary, William's consort William himself, Queen Anne and her husband and George II, lived and died there. George III did not live in the Palace but his family were assigned different apartments; his fourth son, Edward, Duke of Kent and his wife, Victoria of Saxe-Coburg, occupying apartments in the south-eastern block, where their daughter, later Queen Victoria was born and lived until her accession.

Our photograph shows the south front, dating from about 1690–5, rising at the south-east to three stories. The vases that surmount the attic and the brackets of the cornice are the sole and frugal allowance of ornament. The first floor at this end of the building contains the King's Gallery, with its elaborate ceiling painted and enriched by William Kent and a curious map over the fireplace (by Robert Norden, 1694), showing the direction of the wind. Set in irregular shrubbery, the exterior view is attractively homely and placid, the only element of pomp that of the statue of William III, presented by the German Emperor in 1907.

New Square, Lincoln's Inn

The pattern of some of London's most beautiful architecture is to be found in its series of "lawyers' colleges"—which Ben Jonson called "the noblest nurseries of humanity and liberty in the kingdom"—the Inns of Court, comprising Middle Temple, Inner Temple, Gray's Inn and Lincoln's Inn and ranged along the western boundary of the City proper. The name, Lincoln's Inn, has its connection with the fourteenth century and Henry de Lacy, Earl of Lincoln, whose house stood on the site, but an historical survey of its buildings would begin with Tudor times and the "New" Square of our photograph is a series of chambers (which have housed many famous men of law) dating from the late seventeenth century; and, as a wall panel in one wing states, completed in 1694. It was originally called Serle Court, having been built by Henry Serle, one of the Benchers of the Inn. The archway leading into New Square from Carey Street, behind the Law Courts, has appropriately two ornamental panels bearing the arms of Henry de Lacy, Earl of Lincoln and Henry Serle respectively. Though some additions and alterations have been made—a top story added, eighteenth century or modern window sashes put in, it looks now very much as it must have done in the time of William III, its doorways, surmounted by their curved, broken pediments, leading to staircases for the most part original. The garden in the centre was planted in 1845. In its cloistered effect and the happy contrast of its greenery with the dark, rusty tone of its old brickwork, New Square is something between the university college quadrangle and the domestic squares that were later to give such distinction to Bloomsbury.

Bedford Square

Part of the great building programme carried out for the Dukes of Bedford in the eighteenth century, Bedford Square is the most distinguished ornament of Bloomsbury and indeed the most complete and perfect of London squares. It has, superlatively, that air of dignity and "good manners" that belongs to its period. The houses conform to a prevailing design, each side having a central group (one of which is seen in our photograph) stuccoed, pilastered, and with a fine pediment—and a nice contrast of pattern with the mellow brick and the rusticated surrounds to the doorways of the houses on either side. While they have this civilised conformity, the individuality of each appears in the slight variations of the beautiful doorways. An integral part of the square's beauty, also, is the oval garden, with its big plane trees, its copse-like mystery of shrubbery and foliage.

Bedford Square was laid out on a portion of the old slum, or "rookery" of St. Giles, about 1775, probably by the architect, Thomas Leverton (No. 1 was the architect's own house). In the days of George IV and William IV it was "judge-land", a number of judges, barristers and eminent lawyers making their homes there. The celebrated Tory Lord Chancellor, Lord Eldon, lived at No. 6 from 1804 to 1816 (his windows were broken by rioters angered at his opposition to amendments of the Corn Laws). The barrister, who was also a poet, Bryan Waller Procter, lived at No. 25. The millionaire scientist, Henry Cavendish lived at No. 11. In the twentieth century, though a few distinguished residents could once be counted, its domestic population has at last dropped to zero, though its offices are for the most part appropriately those of culture. Through stately windows one may peep into the showroom of a well-known publisher or at the activities of a society for the advancement of some worthy cause. In the aspect of the square as a whole there is nothing to disturb its original and exquisite harmony.

The British Museum

The great museum is closely hemmed in by streets to the east and west; this makes all the more striking the spaciousness of the approach from Great Russell Street to the main entrance and southern façade. Its scale and dignity can be appreciated in relation to the small figures advancing across the forecourt and up the broad flight of steps. The front is 370 feet long, the Ionic columns of the colonnade 45 feet high. The element of the colossal, to be noted in so many London buildings of the nineteenth century, is exemplified in the 800 stones, each weighing from 5 to 10 tons, of which the front is constructed. Not since the days of Trajan or Hadrian, said Professor C. R. Cockerell in 1850, had stones of such magnitude been used.

Designed by the pupil of Sir John Soane, Sir Robert Smirke, in 1823, it was completed by his younger brother, Sydney Smirke, who added the Reading Room with its dome, largest of modern domes, in 1857, the Reading Room occupying what had previously been an open, central quadrangle. The southern range containing the great hall and staircase occupies the exact site of the old Montagu House, the mansion "in the French taste", which, by 1823, had clearly become inadequate, even with extensions, to house the growing collection—the Sloane and Harleian Collections, the Cottonian Library, the antiquities including (1816) the "Elgin Marbles", George III's Library presented by George IV. The classical style of the Smirke building is well fitted to create the mood in which the visitor comes to survey or study the endless treasures of the past within. Sir Richard Westmacott (1775–1856), whose sculpture is so much a part of London's ornament (from the "Achilles" in Hyde Park to the monuments of Westminster Abbey and St. Paul's) carried out the group in the pediment over the Museum's eight-columned portico (1847). Its dusky relief represents the Progress of Civilisation. The colonnade to the west terraces the Director's office, that to the east the southern extremity of the department containing priceless stores of manuscripts: to the eye its total extent is an impressive pattern of light and shade.

B.B.C. and All Souls, Langham Place

Skilfully planned on an awkward site, the modern "Temple of the Arts and Muses" (to quote its dedicatory inscription), Broadcasting House, in its oval bulk looks like the hull of some great ship on land. Designed by Val Myer, built in 1931, it comprises a windowless inner tower, massively constructed of brick, excluding sound and daylight, ventilated and air-conditioned by a modern system, perfect in efficiency and containing its honeycomb of broadcasting studios; library and store-rooms between the floors providing further insulation; and round it an outer ring of seven office floors. It contains, in addition, a full-sized concert hall, a great music library. We look, in the photograph, towards the main entrance, with Eric Gill's symbolic sculpture of the magician Prospero and his servant-spirit, Ariel. Above is the chimeless clock of unfailing accuracy, and by the aerials on the top of the building flutters the Corporation's flag, the design suitably conveying that the B.B.C. "puts a girdle round the earth".

A building so purposeful and modern assorts strangely with the church—All Souls—capriciously designed by John Nash (1824), with the "leviathan" of the 1860s, the old Langham Hotel, the dark "Italian" outline of which is to be seen at the left of our picture. Writing of All Souls, "A German Artist in England" remarked that "of all the mad freaks which ever entered the brain of architect or man to devise, this church far out-Herods all the rest." Two circular temples in one with Corinthian columns topped by an "extinguisher" steeple, it is, to say the least, unorthodox. Even the turn of the street here is due to Nash's capriciousness, for it is related that he thus set Portland Place (in the background) and Regent Street, in a different line, to spite Sir John Langham with whom he had quarrelled. Yet if the view becomes a little fantastic from the variety of its constituents it is at the same time extremely interesting to look at.